Bosworth

Bosworth

The Archaeology of the Battlefield

Richard Mackinder

Foreword by Philippa Langley MBE

Pen & Sword
MILITARY

First published in Great Britain in 2021 by
Pen & Sword Military
An imprint of
Pen & Sword Books Ltd
Yorkshire – Philadelphia

ISBN 978 1 39901 052 8

A CIP catalogue record for this book is
available from the British Library.

Typeset by Mac Style
Printed and bound in India by Replika Press Pvt. Ltd.

Pen & Sword Books Limited incorporates the imprints of Atlas, Archaeology,
Aviation, Discovery, Family History, Fiction, History, Maritime, Military, Military
Classics, Politics, Select, Transport, True Crime, Air World, Frontline Publishing,
Leo Cooper, Remember When, Seaforth Publishing, The Praetorian Press,
Wharncliffe Local History, Wharncliffe Transport, Wharncliffe True Crime
and White Owl.

For a complete list of Pen & Sword titles please contact

PEN & SWORD BOOKS LIMITED
47 Church Street, Barnsley, South Yorkshire, S70 2AS, England
E-mail: enquiries@pen-and-sword.co.uk
Website: www.pen-and-sword.co.uk

Or

PEN AND SWORD BOOKS
1950 Lawrence Rd, Havertown, PA 19083, USA
E-mail: Uspen-and-sword@casematepublishers.com
Website: www.penandswordbooks.com

Contents

Foreword

I first met Richard Mackinder in 2005 when the landmark Bosworth battlefield investigation had begun. Crucial evidence would come from a systematic metal-detecting survey; one of the first of its kind, and in which Richard would play a key role. We weren't to know then, of course, just how successful it would be, and how it's most important find – the silver gilt boar badge – would help change our thinking about the site of this iconic battlefield where a King of England lost his life. The boar badge was found in 2009 by leading detectorist Carl Dawson in the final moments of a search of a field as the final funding was spent. Was it meant to be? I'd like to think so.

In writing this remarkable new book, Richard Mackinder has now brought all of his considerable knowledge and experience to bear, gleaned from his twenty-five years at the Bosworth Battlefield Heritage Centre as a ranger and manager, and as a leading metal detectorist with his team of committed professionals in his Ambion Historical & Archaeological Research Group (AHARG). In December 2015 I was privileged to be asked to join them in a search for the location of Henry Tudor's camp and spent four utterly absorbing days with these leading experts. I was that novice detectorist referred to on p. 7.

In this new work, Richard aims to question with an open mind all that has gone before and, in so doing, to set aside preconceived ideas. He has achieved this aim. In using the finds, landscapes and diverse evidences which are so beautifully presented in this one handy reference guide it offers a fresh perspective for all those interested in the battle and beyond. It also helps probe much of our current mythology in placing Thomas, Lord Stanley at the battle. This is an important step forward. Very few researchers or historians have placed this important question under the spotlight.

Perhaps what is even more remarkable is what this work does in terms of its analysis of the role in the battle of Henry Percy, 4th Earl of Northumberland (1449–89), the commander of King Richard's left flank. A great deal has been written over the centuries about Northumberland's non-participation in the fighting but now evidences are presented that shine a new light on this significant issue. This is another important step forward in our knowledge and understanding of this historic battlefield.

Also brought to light is a new discussion concerning King Richard's final moments, with an analysis of the battle wounds from his remains. Here once again we see an examination that offers a new interpretation; one that helps clarify events, particularly concerning the use of a war hammer. For all those interested in the battle, this is a significant marker that following the king's discovery in 2012 many specialists reached the same or similar conclusion.

Richard Mackinder's exceptional new work now sits as a very important part of the canon into the study of Bosworth – and with the continuing research work of AHARG, we can look forward to more discoveries to come. I commend this work to you.

Philippa Langley MBE
Led the Search for Richard III

Looking at the Evidence – Drafting a Hypothesis

The following has been written to encourage all who read it to question what has gone before, to enter into a discussion with an open mind and to set aside preconceived ideas.

When I was a child, I used to love watching Basil Rathbone as Sherlock Holmes in the old movies. At some point in one of those films he stated those immortal words, 'When you have eliminated the impossible, whatever remains, however improbable, must be the truth.' (Sir Arthur Conan Doyle). As with a lot of things to do with Mr Holmes, most things were black and white (including the films!). I would, however, suggest a more practical saying should be, 'If everything else is found to be unlikely, what is left must be the most likely.' I have tried to look at some of the main aspects around the battle, with no preconceived ideas, to look at the evidence and draw conclusions for what may have happened.

History is fact – only the interpretation keeps changing.

Acknowledgements

My thanks to all of those, too numerous to mention, who have guided, pushed and supported me, especially my family, through the various off-the-wall scenarios that I have come up with, often at 2 o'clock in the morning!

I must also thank the original small band of dedicated metal-detectorists, Pete, Carl, John and Trevor, who have not only spent many hours detecting hectares of fields, but have had the patience to teach me at least the basics of working with a metal detector. These guys make up the core of Ambion Historical & Archaeological Research Group (www.AHARG.co.uk) – a committed group of friends, along with Simon, Malcom, Barry and Roger.

I am hugely grateful to all the landowners whose ground we have been allowed to tramp across over the years. Without their continued support and genuine interest in what we do none of this would have ever happened.

Thanks to Turi and Kevin, for cajoling me to actually undertake this project at all.

Lastly, to my publisher for believing there was a book within the 'ramblings of a madman'.

Richard Mackinder
September 2021

Note: The digital mapping has been fixed to a map base comprising copies of the out-of-copyright first-edition Ordnance Survey 1:10560 maps. Where modern Ordnance Survey has been used in illustrations then appropriate copyright statements have been made in the specific map captions.

All photographs, unless otherwise stated, are copyright of Richard Mackinder.

As for me, I make my prayer to you, O Lord;
at an acceptable time, O God.
Answer me, O God, in the abundance of your mercy
and with your sure salvation.
Draw me out of the mire, that I sink not;
let me be rescued from those who hate me and out of the deep waters.
Let not the water flood drown me, neither the deep swallow me up;
let not the pit shut its mouth upon me.
Answer me, Lord, for your loving-kindness is good;
turn to me in the multitude of your mercies.
Hide not your face from your servant;
be swift to answer me, for I am in trouble.
Draw near to my soul and redeem me;
deliver me because of my enemies.

Psalm 69:14–20

Introduction

Who am I to suggest yet another interpretation of a battle that took place over 500 years ago? There are already many different versions of what might have happened. Some written by scholars, some by historians, and some by people whom I suspect have never even been to the area where we now know at least part of the battle was fought. What follows is my interpretation of information gleaned from recent research, some of which I have been fortunate enough to have been involved in first-hand.

I started working at the Bosworth battlefield site in 1991 as one of a team of four Countryside Rangers who managed a site that was only open to the public from Easter to October each year. As part of our role as staff there, we would take small numbers of school groups around a trail, telling a version of the story based on research that had been undertaken on behalf of Leicestershire County Council by Dr Danny Williams of Leicester University for the opening of the battlefield heritage centre in 1974.

Between early September and the middle of October each year, we would take the school children up to the top of Ambion Hill where we stated, 'Richard III camped on this very field before charging down with a thousand knights'. We would follow the path, heading down towards Shenton village, to the east of where we flew Henry Tudor's flag near Shenton Station (a Victorian railway station). We would then walk on to a nearby small field next to the Ashby de la Zouch Canal and gather by a large stone memorial which read, 'Richard Plantagenet was slain here. 22nd August 1485'. We would then retrace our steps past the station and on into Ambion Wood where we told the children a marsh had once been, and that Henry had skirted this to protect his flank at the beginning of the battle. We would finally return to the battlefield heritage centre via the nineteenth-century stone cairn known as King Dick's Well – allegedly marking the spot where Dickon had his last drink before confronting Henry, Earl of Richmond on that fateful Monday morning in late August 1485.

All of this was always said with the full conviction that we spoke the truth, even though in 1985 someone had *dared* to stand up against the county council and suggest that its interpretation of those events could have been wrong.

Peter Foss agreed with Williams that Richard's camp was at Ambion Hill. However, he placed the marsh to the south of Ambion Hill on the old Roman road known as Fenn Lane, subsequently placing the battle in a different area altogether. His book *The Field of Redemore, The Battle of Bosworth, 1485* is still available to read.

Foss was not alone in suggesting that the council might be wrong. After 1985, a plethora of historians and academics came up with a number of different interpretations and geographical options for the battle. These included, in 2001, Michael Jones, who not only stated the battle was in the wrong place, but in the wrong county. It should have been in Warwickshire, according to his book *Bosworth 1485: Psychology of a Battle*. Despite everything, as with Foss's interpretation, and for whatever reasons, all were dismissed by the county council.

However, along with a growing number of others, I began to question what we were saying to the public. In 1999, while still working for the county council at the site, I set up a small team of volunteers. We called ourselves 'Ambion Historical and Archaeological Research Group' (AHARG). Our brief was simple: to try and understand what had happened on and around the area of Ambion Hill. Our primary period of interest was the Late Medieval period. However, we soon uncovered evidence of man's impact on the landscape from ancient times through to modern times with the railway and canal. We did not know at the time, but this would include evidence of Neolithic man, the Romans, the English Civil War, the Industrial Revolution and, eventually, undisputable evidence for the Battle of Bosworth.

In 2005, following a sizeable National Lottery Heritage Fund grant, the battlefield heritage centre underwent a major update. Some of the grant went towards rebuilding the museum. Other money was used to construct a classroom for the growing number of visiting schoolchildren. However, part of the grant went towards an archaeological survey. This survey was led by a partnership between Leicestershire County Council and the Battlefield Trust. Glenn Ford, the lead archaeologist, led a team of experts – some paid, some volunteers – but all totally professional.

My work on this project since then has taught me many things. One is that we must be careful not to simply base a hypothesis on supposition, rather the facts. Perceived 'facts' must be checked, questioned and, where possible, tested. Only after passing those tests, can the hypothesis be proven, however unlikely it may seem initially; or how it may contradict what was once thought to be true.

Another lesson I learned early on is that one must not assume anything, least of all that solving the numerous riddles about this battle, and these events surrounding it, would be easy!

In January 2016, I left my job with Leicestershire County Council after over twenty years; however, I have continued to work as a volunteer both in the field and coordinating others in the research of this fascinating battle.

The thoughts and ideas that follow are based on my experiences and local knowledge. It is my personal interpretation of what happened during the battle and how I, and initially that small group of people who became my firm friends, set out to find some answers to the relatively simple question, where, and how, was the Battle of Bosworth fought?

Chapter 1

Routes to the Battle

I t is not my place here to talk about the events leading up to the battle, what happened months or years before August 1485. However, some things relating to the battle cannot be separated from what came before.

One question that I have often been asked is why did the battle take place 'here' in the first place? My first hypothesis therefore is in an attempt to answer this seemingly simple question.

We know for a fact that Henry Tudor landed on 7 August with a force of mainly Continental troops, at Mill Bay, near Milford Haven, close to Pembroke Castle where he had been born twenty-eight years before. He then headed virtually unopposed north, up through Wales before he turned south-east, to aim towards the capital, and crossed the River Severn at Shrewsbury. He then proceeded to Stafford, where he met with Sir William Stanley on about 19 August, and from that point his progress slowed considerably, presumably to allow time for further support to arrive. On the evening of 20 August, he and his army arrived at Atherstone. William Stanley had been shadowing Tudor and his army, which had now increased to about 5,000, but as yet the Stanleys had not openly committed to Henry or, indeed, to Richard.

We are then told in some early accounts that Henry was encamped at or near Merevale Abbey some days before the battle, a guest of the abbot. One assumes, if he had been unopposed by Richard, he was planning to carry on in a southerly direction along Watling Street and enter London. However, Henry probably knew this was unlikely to happen, and he certainly could not afford to be caught by an enemy force from the rear. He therefore also knew he would have to meet Richard somewhere and stand and fight.

John Hardwick of nearby Lindley Hall 'advised Henry Tudor on the geography of the battle area and the weather', according to John Austin in his book *Merevale and Atherstone 1485: Recent Bosworth Discoveries*, p. 47. If this was the case, knowing Richard was not far away and the ground looked promising, did Tudor, with the advice of his commanders, force the issue?

We know, as Henry must have, that on the Sunday morning, 21 August 1485, Richard III had been in the city of Leicester, having arrived from Nottingham on the 20th. He would have also heard that Richard subsequently left Leicester, most probably via Bow Bridge, to travel west towards Henry Tudor and his smaller force and encamped somewhere near Sutton Cheney that evening.

To understand how and why the opposing forces camped and eventually met where they did, we must examine the road infrastructure of the late medieval period, which is completely different from that of today. The old Roman roads Watling Street (the modern A5) and Fenn Lane are of major importance in this hypothesis.

Watling Street is the major route from north-west Wales to London, via Atherstone and close by Merevale Abbey. This was Henry's most likely planned route. Fenn Lane is the most direct route from what was then the town of Leicester to Watling Street, transecting the now known eventual battle site. In fact, if one draws a straight line along Fenn Lane, from the village of Fenny Drayton, which sits adjacent to the current A5, to the existing crossroads of Fenn Lane and Shenton Lane just north of the village of Dadlington, one can then extend it straight through the villages of Kirkby Mallory and Peckleton and ultimately along 'King Richard's Road' and across Bow Bridge into the heart of Leicester itself. This, I would suggest, is the most likely route that Richard would have taken.

If one is to believe that the current Fenn Lane is indeed on the line of a Roman road, it went from a fixed point (Leicester) to a linear feature, some 10 miles to the west (Watling Street). As there is a known Roman army camp, called Manduessedum, near Mancetter, approximately 1 mile to the north of the junction between Fenn Lane and Watling Street, why then did the Romans build a road further south, through what has now been proven a marsh, when the most direct route from the camp would have avoided the low-lying marsh altogether?

In 2009 a member of the research team was metal-detecting in a field adjacent to Fenn Lane and saw a polished stone sitting on the surface. A similar stone was then given to the author in 2010 by a local farmer who had found it while ploughing a field a short distance to the east of the earlier find. They turned out to be two polished stone axe heads. These, along with three others found many years before, but unknown to the research team at the time, date from the Neolithic period. Axe heads of this type are known to have been used as offerings, often by being thrown into areas of open water for the gods.

Polished stone axes found adjacent to Fenn Lane in areas of known alluvium deposit. A marsh, or open water, can only be found in areas of alluvium deposit.

I therefore suggest that Neolithic man may have built a (ceremonial?) causeway across the low-lying marshy ground, and subsequently made regular offerings to their 'water gods'. Centuries later, when the Romans later took over the country, and the gods, the populous followed. The paths and causeways were developed from mud tracks and raised wooden causeways over the marshy ground into more substantial stone roads.

The research team even found evidence of a Roman temple that had been built on a nearby hill to overlook the earlier pre-Roman religious sites. This road therefore was probably the primary route from the Roman campsite straddling Watling Street to Ratae Corieltauvorum (Leicester), which in 1485 was still not only there in the landscape but was probably one of the best roads in the area, and Richard and Henry would therefore have logically both used it.

One can still see evidence of the Roman road today, both in the aerial photographs of the area and in the more modern ditches that now cut through the original line of the road.

An aerial photograph showing a series of crop marks on the original Roman road close to the later 1485 battle site.

Chapter 2

Henry's Camp

Tradition places Henry at Merevale Abbey on 20 August, meeting Sir William Stanley who was both his step-uncle and brother-in-law to Margaret Beaufort. He was also one of the richest men in England. In Polydore Vergil's *Historia Anglia* (commissioned by Henry VII in 1505 – only twenty years after the event), he states that Henry and Stanley conferred '... in what sort to arraign battle with King Richard, whom they heard to be not far off'. A native of Urbino, Vergil was an Italian cleric sent to England in 1501 by Pope Alexander VI as a sub-collector of 'Peter's Pence', which was an annual tax of one penny from every householder having land of a certain value, paid to the papal see at Rome.

Modern historian Michael Jones not only agrees with Vergil and states that Henry stayed at the abbey, but that he then subsequently fought in that immediate area.

We know from the *Crowland Chronicle*, a near contemporary source of Vergil, that after the battle 'Compensation Warrants' were issued to Merevale Abbey by the victorious king in November and December of 1485, just three months after the battle. Part of the first warrant reads: '... and to deliver the same [compensation] to certain townships which sustained losses to their corns and grains by us and our company at our late victorious field for our due recompense on our behalf'. The warrant goes on to mention Atherstone, Fenny Drayton, Witherley and Mancetter by name. The abbey was paid 100 marks in cash, with an additional 10 marks a short while later. The town of Atherstone received £24 13s. 4d. to make up for the losses in corn and grain resulting probably from the army trampling through their fields.

In the 1970s, Danny Williams stated in his book *The Battle of Bosworth* that Henry moved east from Merevale after that meeting on the 20th and camped on the eve of the battle at an area known as Whitemoors, situated below Ambion Hill and just south of the village of Shenton. On the back of this statement, Leicestershire County Council rented a small field from the local landowner and created a car park and information point. For many years I raised the Royal Standard for Henry at this site to help reinforce this to the public.

We now know that a major part of the battle took place around the current Fenn Lane Farm, which is further to the south-east of Whitemoors. Therefore, Williams's interpretation for Henry's camp must be wrong. Could it be that Henry and his army stayed *in* the abbey for at least two full days, until the Monday morning, marched a total distance of 9½km (6 miles) by turning south down Watling Street before turning east along Fenn Lane, engaged and defeated a superior force, then finally marched another 16km (10 miles) into Leicester to prove to the world he was the new King of England?

With the help of some reasonably recently gained crucial pieces of information, I now propose a third, alternative theory. Henry may or may not have held a meeting in the abbey curtilage itself but I think it unlikely he and his army camped in the actual grounds of the abbey. The abbey would not have been big enough to house all the men, horses and accompanying accoutrements, but the surrounding villages would have been – hence the recompense. The abbey, however, was given the largest fee. I believe this to be because, even though they may have been within the parish boundaries of Atherstone, Witherley, Mancetter and Fenny Drayton, much of the ground that the army camped on may have been *owned* by the abbey. To prove (or disprove) this, a map needs to be found showing exactly what grounds were owned by the abbey in 1485.

To help support this, Vergil makes the following comment:

After he had wandered about a long while and could not find it, he [Henry] fearfully came to a certain hamlet more than three miles from his camp. So not to fall into a trap, he did not dare ask the way of anybody, and he spent his night there, not so afraid of his present danger as of that yet to come.

To further boost this hypothesis, there is still a 'green lane' that runs from Fenn Lane, east of Fenny Drayton in a north-westerly direction, running close to Witherley and on towards the village of Sheepy Magna. More significantly, there are a number of new pieces of information that have come to light following the initial research undertaken up to 2010:

- The Abbot of Merevale had a summer residence in the north-west of the parish of Sheepy.
- The thirty-fifth roundshot added to the battlefield database was found by an independent detectorist on the north side of the village of Sheepy. It does not seem to have ever been fired.
- Within about 100m from the roundshot, a medieval silver hammered coin was found by the same detectorist. That in itself is not uncommon. This coin however is Portuguese and can be accurately dated to between 1438 and 1481. Very few have ever been recorded in the Midlands.
- 300m to the south, another item was found. This was a buckle that may well have belonged to a medieval spur.

- The last item found in this neighbourhood and of interest to the battle researcher was a late medieval dagger quillon.
- Sheepy is 5km or 3 miles from Merevale – just as Vergil told us!

Roundshot.

An Alfonso V coin.

A possible spur buckle.

A dagger quillon.

A map showing the parishes given recompense in December 1485 with the possible route of a medieval 'green lane' highlighted.

Though the last two artifacts are far from unique, or indeed even uncommon, when put into the context of such a small area, along with a Portuguese coin and a roundshot, I suggest there is something here of major significance.

I therefore propose that Henry was actually billeted at, or at least very near, Sheepy in the abbot's Summer House, while his men were camped in the villages south of Sheepy on, or at least near to, the lane that would ultimately take him towards his final victory.

All four metal-detected finds seen opposite were found by a local amateur metal-detectorist, in a local farmer's private field. Following his work, the research team sought permission and moved into the neighbouring 16-hectare field (40 acres) and undertook a preliminary survey at the now standard 2.5m systematic format. Five working days were spent in the field. This equated to twenty man days by the regular team (along with four days by a complete novice detectorist).

About 12 hectares (30 acres) of stubble were covered by the team and a number of items were recovered. At least 7 of these have proved to be of potential interest, and they include 3 mounts, 2 buckles, 1 belt fitting and 1 button. A potential silver spur fitting might be medieval, but currently it is felt to be more likely post-battle.

Two of these finds have been singled out by Professor Kevin Schurer of Leicester University and identified as heraldic pieces. The first of these is a lead alloy leather fitting or mount. It is a six-pointed star and Professor Schurer has identified the family that would have used this as part of their heraldic device as the Mordaunts.

Sir John Mordaunt was born in 1465. He fought, and was wounded, at the Battle of Barnet (14 April 1471). He was then at Bosworth fourteen years later and eventually was Henry's commander at Stoke Field in 1487. He ultimately became the King's Sergeant, and then followed Reginald Bray as Steward of the Duchy of Lancaster. He was married to Edith Latimer. He is buried in All Saints Church, Turvey, Bedfordshire.

The second fitting or button was a lead Catherine Wheel with either enamel or silver inlaid into the recesses. This has again been identified by Professor Schurer as most likely belonging to one of three candidates: the Manners family, the Babingtons, who both used it at times, or, the most likely candidate, Sir John Scott of Scott's Hall, Smeeth/Brabourne, Kent.

Sir John owned land from Ashford to London, and was a senior member of Edward IV's household, Captain of Calais,

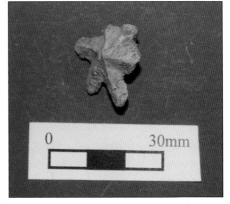

A lead alloy fitting for the household of Sir John Mordaunt.

Warden of the Cinque Ports and later High Sheriff of Kent. His mother was a Herbert and closely connected to the Herberts of Pembroke. He was one of two envoys sent to Brittany to retrieve Henry Tudor in Edward IV's name and acted as ambassador there too. He was a strong supporter of Richard III, until at least 1484. The question is, did he change sides before Bosworth? The family certainly thrived after 1485. Sir John died on 17 October 1485 and is buried in St Mary the Virgin Church, Brabourne, Kent.

A copper alloy fitting for the household of Sir John Scott of Scott's Hall.

There is strong evidence that Henry visited areas that were at least 'part of Merevale'. This is based on both written accounts (Vergil and the *Crowland Chronicle*) and recent identified finds from a systematic survey.

What do we know about the abbey? Merevale Abbey was founded in 1148 by Robert *de Ferrers*, 2nd Earl of Derby. Agnes Ferrers was born 300 years later, in 1438. She was the only child of Elizabeth Bealknap and Sir William de Ferrers, 6th Baron Ferrers of Chartley. Agnes married Sir Walter Devereux sometime before 1446. Thus, Anne was at most 7 years of age at her marriage – Sir Walter was no more than 14 years, having been born in 1432.

Like his father before him, Walter Devereux was a Yorkist. He was with the Duke of York at the Battle of Ludford Bridge on 12 October 1459, but surrendered and threw himself on the king's mercy. Granted his life, he was condemned to forfeit his lands, and they were awarded to Humphrey Stafford, Earl of Stafford. He later redeemed his properties for a fine of 500 marks. He fought at the Battle of Towton on 29 March 1461, where he was knighted. As a Yorkist, Devereux held many offices under Edward IV. He was appointed on 18 June 1463 as Constable of Aberystwyth Castle for life, and on 10 August 1464 joint keeper of 'le heywode' in Herefordshire.

Walter Devereux fought at the Battle of Barnet on 14 April 1471 and at the Battle of Tewkesbury on 4 May 1471 where Edward IV secured his throne. He was one of the Lords who swore in the Parliament Chamber at Westminster on 3 July 1471 to accept Edward, Prince of Wales, as heir to the Crown, and selected on 20 February 1472 as a tutor and councillor until the prince reached the age of 14 years. On 26 July 1461 Walter Devereux was raised to the rank of baron in right of his wife and on account of his great services against Henry VI, the Duke of Exeter, the Earls of Pembroke and Wiltshire, and the other rebels and traitors, thereby becoming Lord Ferrers.

Walter Devereux supported Richard III of England during his reign, and fought on his side at Bosworth in the vanguard under John Howard, Duke of Norfolk, alongside Sir Robert Brackenbury and Thomas Howard, Earl of Surrey. Devereux was slain during the initial fight.

Since the family seem to have such a strong Ricardian connection, the question that needs to be answered is why did Tudor even consider stopping at Merevale in the first place? Assuming we have the correct fields (and certainly the finds would suggest we might), there could be an alternative explanation.

Lynne Percival and Jim Beechey of Sheepy Local History Society have been researching the possible ownership of the fields off Orton Lane. They have traced back as far as 1764 when a survey was carried out of the farms and lands belonging to the Revd Thomas Gresley and Miss Hannah Vincent, and there are documents at the record office in relation to these families (filed under DE5871 and include around 146 documents relating to Sheepy, with the earliest dated *c.* 1247). The search-room list states:

> The Vincent family began acquiring lands in Sheepy Magna and the surrounding parishes around the end of the 15th century. After the Dissolution, their holdings were considerably augmented by the grant of the manor of Sheepy Magna to Robert Vincent in 1544. The extensive estates passed to the Gresley family with the marriage of Elizabeth Vincent to Thomas Gresley of Netherseal in 1757.

Lynne and Jim are currently still of the opinion that the Vincents acquired land from Ranton Priory after the Dissolution; and not Merevale Abbey.

What do we know about Ranton? According to Historic England:

THE AUGUSTINIAN PRIORY OF RANTON
The priory of Ranton was founded about the mid-12th century by Robert fitz Noel of Ellenhall, whose father had been granted Ranton in fee by Nicholas de Stafford. The foundation charter states that the canons of Ranton were living 'under the rule and obedience' of Haughmond Abbey (Salop.), and this helps to fix the date of foundation. Ranton must have been founded after the establishment of the mother-house at Haughmond (between 1130 and 1138) and by 1166 when some of the witnesses to the foundation charter were dead.

The founder's son, Thomas Noel, added land in Bridgeford (in Seighford), Ranton, and Coton Clanford and arranged to be buried in the priory. The land in Bridgeford, however, was detained by his daughter and coheir, Alice, and her husband, William de Harcourt. Eventually, in her widowhood, Alice regranted this land to the priory with her own body for burial and added more land from her demesne of Seighford. Richard de Harcourt of Great Sheepy (Leicestershire) gave the priory 9 virgates of land in Great Sheepy with fishing rights and 2*s.* rent from his mill there; this property was the priory's most important temporal estate outside Staffordshire.

Ranton was to have complete independence from Haughmond in all matters spiritual and temporal, but a 'customary payment' of 100*s.* was to be made to Haughmond each year. It is not clear how these events affected the rights of the Harcourt family who in 1209 possessed what was described as the advowson of Ranton. The family, however, evidently exercised the right of confirming elections throughout the rest of the priory's history.

A medieval coin, a soldino of an uncertain doge but probably dates from between 1367 and 1423 due to the reverse having an inner circle.

What makes this option of the landowner more interesting is the fact that the Harcourts were Tudor supporters. Indeed, Sir Robert Harcourt may well have been Henry's banner bearer at Bosworth, after the death of Sir William Brandon. So, if we have the right area, which church (if either) owned it? Only further research may answer this question.

To back up the suggestion that the area immediately around the village of Sheepy was the campsite of Henry – or at least some of his senior commanders – there is an interesting find logged on the Portable Antiquities Scheme (PAS) database. Not only are there two finds which can be linked to two individuals we know were present during the battle, but we have two foreign coins – one Italian and one Portuguese. The value of a medieval hammered coin is not in what (or even who) is stamped on the face – but the amount of silver in the coin. However, what are two foreign coins doing in this backwater, when we know that there were foreign soldiers preparing to fight a battle? Coincidence can surely only be taken so far.

Henry Tudor, Earl of Richmond.

Chapter 3

The 'Battle' Before the Battle

E veryone recounts the events around 22 August 1485 correctly – or otherwise. However, an event that is often overlooked took place on 20 August 1485. For on this day, we are told by the ballads written for Thomas Stanley (and after the execution of his brother Sir William in 1495), there was 'some' military activity by Lord Stanley, but they only insinuate what form this took.

What we are told is that Richard Broughton, Sherriff of Warwickshire and Leicestershire, was killed on that day probably fighting against Henry's forward troops. 'An incident strangely ignored', says W.E. Hampton in 'Opposition to Henry Tudor after Bosworth'. Mike Ingram, in his book *Bosworth 1485*, says Richard's advanced guard clashed with Henry or Stanley's men and six were killed on that Saturday, two days before the final event which led to the death of king.

Chris Skidmore, in his book *Bosworth – the Birth of the Tudors*, gives us a little more detail:

> There may be some truth behind there being some kind of initial skirmish, if not several, taking place during the night of 20 August and the early morning of the 21st. if later inquisitions post mortem are taken at face value, Richard Broughton, the sheriff of Warwickshire and Leicestershire, is recorded as having died on 20 August, John Kebell of Rearsby in Leicestershire on the 21st; both were prominent Leicestershire figures who had been retainers of Lord Hastings, but had continued to serve Richard as JPs. A sperate group of men, from around the Essex area, are also recorded as having died on 20 or 21 August, including John Cock of Chadwell St Mary in Essex, who died on the 20th, William Curson of Brightwell in Suffolk, who died on the 21st, Thomas Hampden of Great Hampden in Buckinghamshire but who also owned lands at Theydon Mount in Essex died on the same day, as did William Joyce, who may have been the same person as William Joys of Halesworth in Suffolk. None of these men held any office under Richard, but they did all live near to Castle Hedingham in Essex, the ancestral home of John, Earl of Oxford. Could these men, making their way to join Oxford in Henry's camp, have been intercepted by loyal enforcers of Richard's regime along the way?

Can we work out – or at least suggest an area geographically, where this may have happened?

If we are correct about where Henry's forces were before the 20th – and we know that Richard, and the bulk of his forces did not leave Leicester until (the morning of Sunday) the 21st, can we assume that Broughton and his small group of riders had been in Leicester as well before setting out to either join Henry as deserters of Richard or as loyal supporters of the king, and were in fact trying to ascertain both the lie of the land and the layout of all the opposing forces?

Either way, if Broughton moved towards Henry's 'suspected' position from Leicester, he would move west towards Tamworth/Atherstone or even Lichfield and would quiet easily go via Desford, Market Bosworth and Wellsborough heading for Watling Street between Atherstone and Tamworth. Did the two opposing forces collide somewhere along that road?

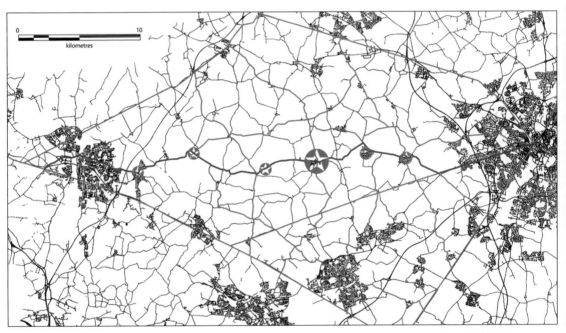

A map showing the possible route from Leicester to the A5 via Market Bosworth (in blue). Other assumed major routes in purple.

Little known work has been carried out along this road. Certainly nothing in a consistent formal manner such as AHARG undertakes currently, however some finds have been reported over the years to the PAS. These finds can then be further analysed to see if they are from the correct period, and subsequently which might be from the skirmish, or at least from people who were involved in some way in that skirmish. Once identified, these need to be plotted using a mapping programme to try to ascertain if there are any abnormal concentrations or patterns.

The PAS was set up in Britain following the passing of the Treasure Act in July 1996. This Act replaced the medieval law of treasure trove in England and Wales. The Treasure Act gave some protection to certain archaeological finds, although a great many other objects were being found by members of the public that did not fall into the category of 'treasure' but were nonetheless important to understand the fuller picture of both the archaeology and the history of a site.

Some people had before this date taken (some of) their finds to local museums to record them, but it was quickly realised that many more objects were simply never recorded. These unrecorded and unprovenanced finds meant a huge loss of knowledge, which in many ways was irreplaceable. The general response to this was that the recording of all archaeological finds was important and that a consistent voluntary scheme to record finds should be established.

In December 1996 the then Department of National Heritage (now the Department for Digital, Culture, Media & Sport (DCMS)) provided funding for a two-year programme of six pilot schemes, starting in September 1997. There were six Finds Liaison Officers (FLO) employed, and this was coordinated and funded by the British Museum.

The FLO's job was to be the first point of contact for the finders, to record finds and provide further information on the finds. The FLO was also there to advise on best practice, such as over cleaning, treasure law or work on Scheduled Monuments. Initially the FLOs recoded any finds on their own individual databases – some of which were paper based! It was soon realised that this needed to change and a more comprehensive and standardised system for recording finds was certainly required.

In July 1999 a new database was designed and made web-based. Within the first 12 months over 13,500 objects were recorded.

The scheme continues to grow and now consists of a network of:

- Nearly forty FLOs.
- A part-time illustrator.
- Six Finds Advisers.
- An ICT Adviser.
- A Resources Manager (formerly administrator).
- A Deputy Head.
- The Head of Portable Antiquities & Treasure.

The work of the scheme is supported by many temporary assistants and volunteers, working with FLOs and Finds Advisers. Following a review conducted by the Museums, Libraries and Archives Council (or MLA), the aims of the scheme were revised and are summarised here.

Aims and Objectives

The PAS is a partnership project which records archaeological objects found by the public in order to advance our understanding of the past. The scheme achieves this through:

- Promoting maximum public interest and benefit from the recovery, recording and research of portable antiquities.
- Promoting best practice by finders/landowners and archaeologists/museums in the discovery, recording and conservation of finds made by the public.
- Partnership with museums and others, raising awareness among the public, including young people, of the educational value of recording archaeological finds in their context and facilitating research in them.
- Creating partnerships between finders and museums/archaeologists to increase participation in archaeology and advancing our understanding of the past.
- Supporting the Treasure Act, and increasing opportunities for museums to acquire archaeological finds for public benefit.

The data gathered by the scheme is published on an online database (www.finds. org.uk).

In order to fulfil the aims of the scheme staff have to:

- Maintain an online database and promote it as a resource for education and research.
- Hold outreach events, such as finds days, attend metal-detecting club meetings and give talks to national and local group and societies.
- Facilitate displays of finds recorded by the Scheme in museums and elsewhere.
- Help finders to fulfil their obligations under the Treasure Act.
- Publish an annual report and other publications in print and online.

Any analysis of the PAS must therefore be seen in a fair light. As good as the PAS is, it is only as good as the people who sign up to it. It is still not a compulsory scheme and some people who metal-detect unfortunately still do not always notify the FLOs and subsequently these records are not a true account of all the finds recovered. Another reason that these records are not an accurate data set for the battle researcher is that what we are often looking at is the concentration of finds that could be described as low status. Some people will report the 'bright, gilded, high-status' finds such as heraldic pendants or spurs, but do not bother with the more mundane strap ends or buckles. This is extremely frustrating as most of the people who were involved in the events of 1485 were the 'common people' whose only pieces of metal were those same mundane strap ends or buckles. Relatively few people could afford the wealthy items, and those that could – and lost their lives – would often have those pieces recycled – the spoils of war.

Another point to remember when looking at the data is that it is not known how effectively the ground has been detected and so if the find was a purely random one.

Most detectorists search a field in an entirely indiscriminate way, wandering wherever their fancy takes them, often until they find a 'nice piece' when they then hover in that area for a long time in the hope that where there is one there might be more. Usually there is nothing in the immediate area and subsequently this means that people will often say that there is nothing in that field – 'I only found one hammered coin', however, 95 per cent of the field has actually *not* been searched at all.

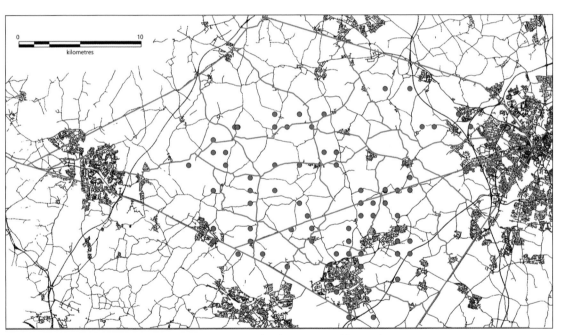

A map showing all medieval finds from the PAS database as of September 2019.

It is also never recorded which fields have been looked in and which ones have not. It would not be the first time that that one hammered coin found was in the corner of a field and low and behold another coin or purse bar was found over the hedge in the adjoining field. That one random find then becomes more significant as part of a more 'major loss' rather than simply a 'random loss'.

All of that said, some useful interpretation can be done from this underutilised data. Further analysis of this data could look at specific type of finds. For example, if we only look at heraldic objects can we identify specific (or at least potential) families and ask the question why might those finds have been lost in that particular vicinity that were then eventually found hundreds of years later. In other words – was it a local family using a regular route so that one might expect items to be lost over a long period of time. Or was it a 'foreign' family (non-local) who had been undertaking a single journey such as to a major church on a pilgrimage. Or was it possibly a person (already known – or not) who took part in the battle.

If it is the latter, it is still not conclusive proof that the object found today was actually lost yesterday in anything more than an accidental loss, as opposed to a conflict with an 'enemy'. Though it certainly may warrant further investigation by more intense fieldwork.

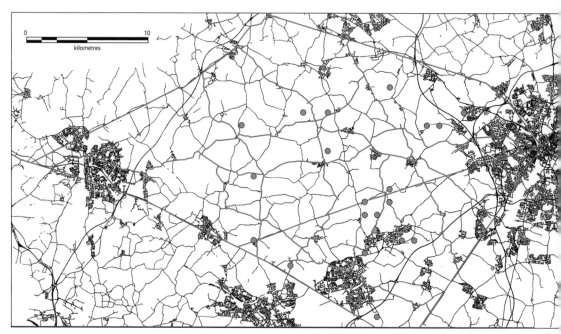

A map showing some of the medieval heraldic finds from the PAS database as of September 2019. These may be significant or not.

When one looks in more detail it is apparent that some of these are unlikely to be related to anyone who may have been involved in the events of August 1485. Knowing that not all finds are recorded, and, as previously stated, in some cases because they are not deemed worthy enough, or worse, they are too good (in the finder's eye), there is one other downside to this data, and that is that some of those finds that are listed in the PAS have no accurate find spot. This is of course sometimes undertaken by the FLO to protect the potential site from improper detecting; and sometimes because the finder might want to keep 'their site' to themselves. However, at least for the time being, it does not help us identify any patterns in the distribution.

We may not have accurate records as to who fought in the skirmish before the main battle on 22 August, but we can assume that there were small forces of mixed personnel. This may have included knights, men-at-arms and possible archers. What we do not know is if they were relatively fast-moving, mounted troops or a slower moving mixture of mounted and foot troops.

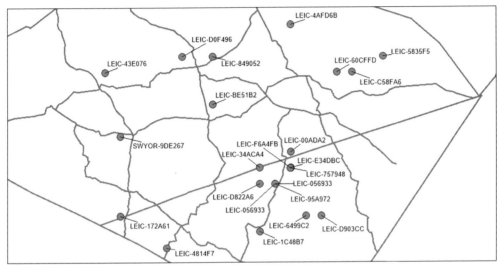

A map showing the locations of some of the heraldic finds from the PAS database as of September 2019.

If Broughton led Richard's force and clashed with Stanley's troops, unless there was a total massacre, Richard would have been given confirmation about Stanley changing sides. There would have been no cry of treason because Richard would have expected Sir William's behaviour and therefore attacking Henry as early as possible would be his only strategy. Reach him and kill him before Stanley fights against you.

The most likely finds that could be related to either the main battle on the 22nd or, more importantly, the skirmish on or around the 20th/21st are listed in the table on the following pages.

Find Number	Find Type	Find Subtype	Notes	Image
SWYOR-9DE267	Pendant	Harness pendant	The arms of the Earls of Lancaster.	
LEIC-D0F496	Mount		Foliate motif surrounded by a blue enamel field.	
LEIC-BE51B2	Stud		Decorated with a man on horseback riding right.	
LEIC-849052	Mount		With a 'Maltese'-style cross and a line of raised triangles.	
LEIC-34ACA4	Chape	Dagger chape	Ornate red lion standing in a white border of a six-petalled flower.	

Find Number	Find Type	Find Subtype	Notes	Image
LEIC-757948	Mount		A zoomorphic animal head form.	
LEIC-4AFD6B	Pendant	Harness pendant	White enamel in the form of a lion/ big cat.	
LEIC-00ADA2	Pendant	Harness pendant	Diagonal blue enamel separating animal lions? The Bohun arms?	
LEIC-60CFFD	Pendant	Harness pendant	Contains a lion passant surrounded by red enamel.	
LEIC-5835F5	Seal matrix		Roger of Trafford, one bird of prey swooping on another. Above this is a left-facing swastika. S'ROGERI OE TRAFFORD+.	

Find Number	Find Type	Find Subtype	Notes	Image
LEIC-172A61	Seal matrix	Pendant seal	War horse and rider. The die shows a Lamb and Flag.	
LEIC-4814F7	Mount		Dog-headed mount.	
LEIC-D822A6	Mount	Harness hook	In the form of a dog.	
LEIC-056933	Seal matrix		'Seal of Ernold'.	

Find Number	Find Type	Find Subtype	Notes	Image
LEIC-6499C2	Pendant	Horse harness	Shield-shaped. Decorated with five left-facing 'rook-like' birds which are surrounded by red enamel. The birds are divided into two rows, three at the top and two at the bottom.	
LEIC-D903CC	Pendant	Harness pendant	Scutiform (shield-shaped), two fields of blue enamel with a diagonal band in its centre, running from top left to bottom right (a bend cotised). The upper right panel has a small patch of gilding.	

(Courtesy of the British Museum's Portable Antiquities Scheme)

Further analysis needs to be undertaken to see if any or all of the items listed can be accurately identified with specific individuals or families that are known to have been involved.

One object is instantly interesting, however, and that is the pendant SWYOR-9DE267 (the arms of the Earls of Lancaster) which was found a short distance south of the (modern) road between Henry's potential campsite and Market Bosworth. (There is at least one strap end and one chape along this same road as well.) Can we identify any of Stanley's forces from the few heraldic finds we so have far? Can we undertake some formal systematic detecting along the Wellsborough Road and find any more concrete evidence for this precursor to the main battle?

Heraldic pendant for the Earls of Lancaster. (*Courtesy of the British Museum's Portable Antiquities Scheme*)

Chapter 4

Richard's Camp

M ost historians (and therefore, most people) put Richard on Ambion Hill, where the current battlefield heritage centre lies, and where his Battle Standard has been flown for the last forty years. This placing has been based primarily on the work of one historian. Raphael Holinshed, in his *Chronicle of England*, published in 1577, stated that, 'King Richard pitched his field on a hill called Anne Beame, refreshed his souldiers and took his rest'. However, just because this statement does not seem to have been directly questioned, it does not necessarily mean that it is fact.

Ambion Hill, as we know it today, is in fact not really a hill at all. It is the end of a curved ridge that runs in an inverted C in an approximate north-west/ south-east direction and is said to be named after a deserted medieval village called Ambion. The first known record for Ambion is 1261, in the Curia Regis Rolls. However, these particular records have not, to my knowledge, been fully searched. The last known record for Ambion was a grant issued to the village for 'the right to warren' (to keep and catch rabbits) in 1347. The assumption could be that at its peak, the village was of reasonable size and well established. Subsequently the 'right to warren' may have been granted because the village was struggling, and possibly died out all together in 1348/9 with the arrival of the Black Death.

In an article called 'Life in a Medieval Village', Linda Alchin states:

The peasants, including serfs, freemen and villeins, on a manor lived close together in one or more villages. Their small, thatch-roofed, and one-roomed houses would be grouped about an open space (the 'green'), or on both sides of a single, narrow street. The only important buildings were the parish church, the parsonage (vicarage), a mill, if a stream ran through the manor, and possibly a blacksmith's shop. The population of one of these villages often did not exceed one hundred people.

There is no record of Ambion having a church, so should we actually call it a village at all? A more accurate term might be that of a hamlet. As in medieval England, the definition of a hamlet tends to be a cluster of houses or dwellings, *without* a church. They are often formed around a single source of economic activity such as a farm, mill, mine or harbour that employed its working population. In this case, a farm with a few small dwellings scattered nearby, at the end of a ridge, and about 1.7km (1 mile) from the 'parent village' of Sutton Cheney might make more sense.

If one looks at different editions of the Ordnance Survey maps for the area, such as the 1835 edition, or those up to at least the 1950s, Richard III's campsite is often marked on the map. It can be found just south of the village of Stapleton, some 3km (2 miles) south-east of the battlefield heritage centre. The triangular field at this location is often marked on maps as 'Bradshaw's'.

The tithe map for this area, dated 1835, has a completely different name for this triangular field; but does, however, name two nearby fields as 'Nether Bradshaw' and 'Over Bradshaw'. The location of these two fields is next to a farm (still in existence today) called Bradshaw Farm. On the first edition of the Ordnance Survey of the same year one can clearly see Ambion Hill marked in those same Bradshaw fields, 3km south-east of where it is stated to be today. Is this a cartographer's mistake or is this indeed the true site of Ambion Hill – even if not the medieval village.

In trying to answer the question of where Richard camped, the location of a site called Ambion could be confusing or indeed somewhat irrelevant. What we do know is that Richard headed out of Leicester at the head of his army on the Sunday morning.

I suggest that Richard took the Roman road to where it breasted the summit of the ridge between the two villages of Sutton Cheney and Stapleton, as looking west he would have had a view of the immediate countryside below the ridge. Scrutinising once more the distribution map of the heraldic finds from the PAS data, it can be

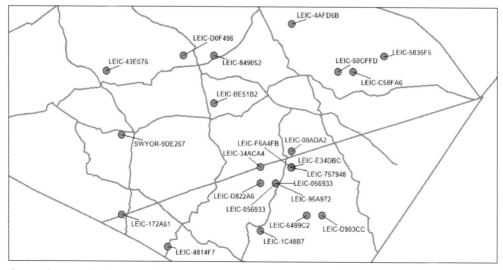

A map showing the locations of some of the heraldic finds from the PAS database as of September 2019.

seen that there are a number of finds along the line of the Roman road. Potentially, Richard may have even been able to see some of the campfires of Henry's men on the horizon, depending on where exactly these camps were. There was no more tactical advantage to be gained by dragging all of his men off the best arterial road, across fields with standing crops, ready for harvest, to camp right at the end of a ridge (modern-day 'Ambion Hill' and the location of the battlefield heritage centre).

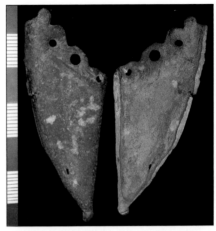

A dagger chape with ornate red lion standing in a white border of a six-petalled flower.

I therefore surmise that Richard set camp with his forces to both the north and south, immediately straddling either side of the road, something which the archaeological evidence is beginning to indicate. He himself may have moved into the relative comfort of the manor house at Sutton Cheney, which was located immediately north of the church, or, as tradition has it, set up his own Royal Tent. His men possibly found spaces on the adjacent land back through the village of Sutton Cheney, and towards the road and beyond, all along the ridge towards the current Bradshaw Farm.

A harness pendant with diagonal blue enamel separating animal (lions?). The Bohun arms?

Given that Richard's camp would have undoubtedly been sacked by the victors after the battle, one would expect to find some archaeological evidence, however faint. There are less than a handful of medieval finds from the end of the ridge (Ambion Hill) after a massively intensive search of the fields by metal-detectorists.

However, on a very much less intensive search, several finds have been collected from fields surrounding the village of Sutton Cheney and the line of the old road. Some of these could be interpreted as 'village litter', or pieces one might associate with a medieval village. They could have been dropped by people throughout the medieval period simply using the road to travel back and forwards to Leicester. Nevertheless, some are more obviously high status or even military, and therefore less likely to have been from the village, nor are they directly from the line of the road (or immediately adjacent to its line) and are therefore, I would suggest, more likely from Richard's camp.

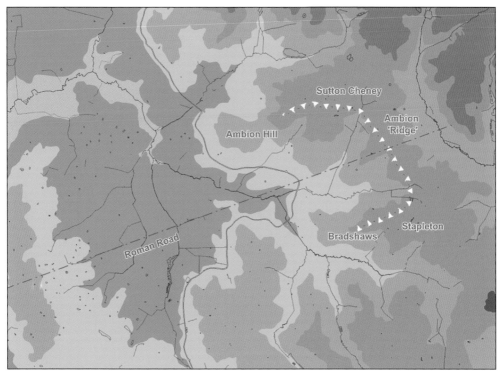

A topographical map showing the ridge running from the villages of Sutton Cheney to Stapleton.

To support my argument, it has been a village tradition that Richard went to hear Mass on the Sunday evening at Sutton Cheney. This has been disputed by some academics as a Victorian invention. Along with this, there is a less well publicised statement that Richard instead went to Mass in the church in the village of Stapleton.

Since verbal traditions are often founded on fact, it is possible, or indeed likely, that it was not Richard himself hearing Mass in either of those churches, as he would have most probably had his own priest, but some of Richard's *men*, who, far from home and facing an uncertain future, decided on the Lord's Day to seek solace in the nearest house of God, and to make their peace with Him? Is it simply the case that 'men of Richard's army went to church' has been shortened over the centuries to simply 'Richard went to church'?

It is also sometimes easier to look at the negative. Is there any logical reason why something is unlikely to be correct or true? One reason I believe the site of the current battlefield heritage centre is an unlikely possible campsite for Richard is simply that there would not be an adequate water supply. At best, there are only potentially a couple of wells in the area dating back to this period, and certainly no known open water courses. This is nowhere near sufficient for a tired, thirsty army of men and horses who have marched 10 miles or more even in a 'English summer'!

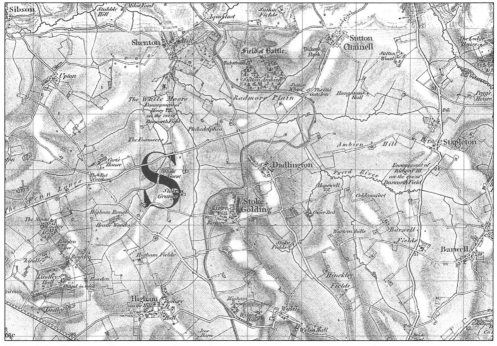

Part of the Ordnance Survey map of 1836. (*Copyright © Cassini Publishing Ltd*)

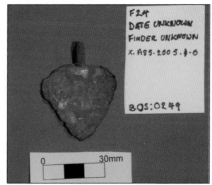

Left: A riveted buckle probably from a piece of armour. *Right*: A gilded horse harness pendant. Both objects were found close to the village of Sutton Cheney.

Any horseman would have major concerns because water consumption is always of great importance, and is critical in avoiding colic impaction, dehydration and other life-threatening ailments in horses. The average horse will consume between 5 and 10 gallons of water a day. A horse deprived of feed, but supplied with drinking water, can survive twenty to twenty-five days. A horse deprived of water may only live for five days.

Going back to the ridge and the old Roman road and looking at the map above, one can see that there is a major water course running just north of the village of

Stapleton. This water course runs west towards Shenton and on further towards Sibson. There are also a number of smaller tributaries that run from the north and flow into the Tweed River. This would allow a far larger number of people (and their horses) to camp on or certainly very close to the ridge, and between the villages of Sutton Cheney and Stapleton.

Reconsidering the discussion of the position of Ambion, as already stated it was recorded as Anabein (*c.* 1270), Anne Beame in Holinshed's *Chronicles of England* (1577), Anbein (1622) and Amyon by John Hutton (1788). According to Eilert Ekwall in his book *The Concise Oxford Dictionary of English Place Names*, the name seems to be derived from the Old English Āna-bēam, a one-beam bridge, probably the hamlet's means of crossing a stream. As we have seen, there are no streams around the current battlefield heritage centre. However, there is the already mentioned stream to the north of Stapleton and one, the Tweed River, to the south.

The battlefield heritage centre may not be in exactly the correct spot as far as the battle of 1485 is concerned, however, it is still definitely worth a visit. It contains an award-winning exhibition with a number of galleries which include an area showing excellent replicas of various hand weapons as well as an area displaying actual archaeological finds from the battle site. The finds include some of the horse-harness pendants, buckles and other paraphernalia connected with this event. As

The Battlefield Sundial.   Richard III, King of England.

well as these more 'common' finds, there is a number of unique finds – including (at least some of) the 'Bosworth Roundshot'.

While the battlefield heritage centre may not be the heart of the battlefield – as first thought in the early 1970s when it opened, it can certainly be described as the 'Gateway to the Battle'. It also commemorates those of all sides who fought and died at the battle with a peaceful marker and sundial, along with two large replica battle standards of Richard and Henry. This is situated at the end of the ridge overlooking the true site of the battle.

Chapter 5

To Battle

The morning of Monday, 22 August 1485 would probably have seen both armies rising before dawn and making final preparations for battle. It has been suggested by many that Richard wore his crown, or diadem, and rode his charger in front of his men to both encourage them and to show them he was the true king and that their cause was just. Whether or not this is true, and it is suggested in *The Great Chronicle* that he probably did, is unlikely ever to be proven but I suspect that Richard himself would have certainly led his troops down the Roman road, probably ten or fifteen men across, as they stretched back as far as the camp on the ridge.

Today a public footpath crosses Fenn Lane, leading from the small village of Dadlington in the south to the equally small village of Shenton in the north (and parallel to the current Shenton Lane), at approximately 88m above sea level. I believe that Richard, having travelled about 3km (or 2 miles) from his camp, turned right at this point and moved off the main road onto a secondary road that was possibly no more than a farm track. As Richard's camp was 116m above sea level this is a fall of some 28m in 2.7km. The footpath then drops a further 3m to a height of only 85m above sea level, as it moves north off the road. At this point, there is a ridge which would have been in front (to the west) of Richard, rising some 4m above his current position, thus rendering him invisible to his enemy situated some distance off. This was of major importance to Richard, as it meant he could now deploy his men into the three main battalia, out of sight of Henry and his men.

What else do we habitually get told about the lead-up to the battle? One often mentioned episode is that of Richard having a last drink at a well before engaging Henry, and many tourists have been shown this location over the years. In 1813 Dr Samuel Parr had a stone cairn built in the corner of a field near the 'summit' of Ambion Hill. In the memoirs of his life and writings, edited by John Johnstone (p. 633), there is the following description:

> We dug, and found things as he [Samuel Parr] had described them; and having ascertained the very spot, we rolled in the stones, and covered them with earth. Now Lord Wentworth and some other gentlemen mean to fence the place with some strong stones, and put a large stone over it, with an inscription, – and you may tell the story if you please.

The monument known as 'King Dick's Well', built in 1813 and situated on Ambion Hill.

In the back of the recess there is a Latin inscription which states:

AQVA. EX HOC. PVTEO HAVSTA SITIM. SEDAVIT RICHARDVS TERTIVS REX ANGLIAE CVM HENRICO COMITE DE RICHMONDIA. ACERRIME. ATQVE. INFENSISSME. PRAELIANS ET. VITA. PARITER AC. SCEPTRO ANTE. NOCTEM. CARITVRVS II. KAL. SEPT. AD MCCCCLXXXV.

Richard III, King of England, slaked his thirst with water drawn from this well when engaged in most bitter and furious battle with Henry, Earl of Richmond, and before being deprived of both his life and his sceptre on the morning of 22 August AD 1485.

This added weight to the story that Richard both camped on Ambion Hill, and that he fought the battle on its slopes.

However, we now know that this is not a place that Richard seems to have ever been. So, was there another well anywhere close to this newly proposed area? On an old map belonging to the Shenton Estate, and about 500m to the west of where I think Richard drew his troops in preparation for battle, a well is indeed marked. Could *this* be the true spot from which he took his last drink? Unfortunately, this well no longer exists – or at least not above ground.

As can be seen in the map opposite, today the modern footpath (in purple) runs nearly north–south, and immediately to the right of Apple Orchard Farm before crossing Fenn Lane. The parallel lines on the extreme right of this map are the embankment supporting the now-disused Victorian railway line. Apple Orchard

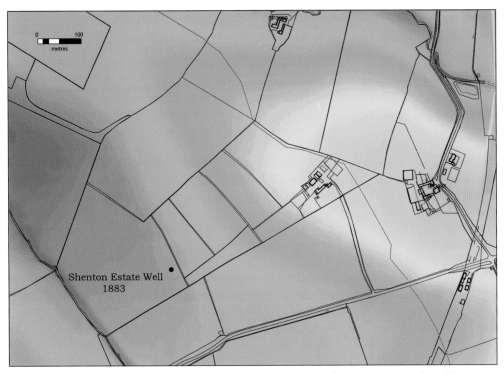

Map showing the more likely well that Richard and his troops might have drawn water from. The lowest area is shown in dark blue and the highest part of the ridge in orange. A stream is marked in purple.

Farm and Lodge Farm can be clearly seen sitting on the ridge with lower ground both to the west and the north-east – where Richard drew his men up out of sight of Henry. The spring has also been marked, some 385m from Apple Orchard Farm – which is, significantly, 5.8m higher than surrounding ground.

Richard's main battalia were led by Norfolk on the northern flank, Northumberland on the southern flank and Richard himself in the centre. Once ready, Richard, I would suspect, would then have waited for Henry to arrive at the field. Henry would have left Sheepy in the early morning to travel the 6km to the site via the 'green lane', effectively collecting his troops as he drew closer. He would have slowly climbed from the initial height of only 74m above sea level to 104m some 5km from Sheepy, and only 1km from where I propose he drew up his men in their battalia, in preparation for the battle to come. Richard, however, and the majority of his men, would still have been invisible to all, or at least to Henry and the vast majority of his smaller number of troops.

Richard now moved his three battalia forward some 600m towards the top of the ridge, where he also probably deployed his gun. The two armies were some 1,700m apart, and ready for battle. Potentially only Richard and Henry's scouts would know exactly where each other's troops were. (Although I suspect if my positioning of Sir William Stanley is correct, 'stood betwixt the armies, and overlooking the field'; he may well have been able to see precisely where all the companies were, on both sides.)

In his book *Bosworth 1485: Psychology of a Battle*, Michael Jones makes an obvious, but an often completely overlooked, statement: 'Nowhere was Death more present than on the battlefield. It could strike without warning at the ordinary solider or captain, or at an army's commander.' He goes on to quote the chronicler Philippe de Commynes, who gives a graphic account of the appalling chaos of hand-to-hand, close-quarter fighting. He bases his knowledge on his first-hand experience gained at the Battle of Montlhéry, between French and Burgundian forces in 1465.

De Commynes fought alongside Charles, Count of Charolais, a young and somewhat reckless commander who, after a number of daring cavalry charges, became separated from the main body of his army. This was further compounded when their small band of mounted men chased a body of enemy foot soldiers. During this rout, one of the enemy pikeman suddenly stopped, turned and stood his ground. The pikeman was quickly overpowered and killed, but not before his pike struck Charolais's breastplate with such force that the count's stomach was marked for some days after the battle.

De Commynes goes on to tell us that minutes later he found himself surrounded by an enemy group of horsemen. His standard bearer was brutally killed while others of his escort were also overwhelmed. As the count fought furiously he was wounded several times, including a blow to the throat that left him scarred for the rest of his life. He goes on to say that the count was only saved from certain death by a rather fat knight who rode between him and his opponents.

De Commynes had witnessed the fog of war first-hand. His ride with the count left him on such an adrenaline high that he did not have time to be frightened. He had viewed the near death of his friend as if he was detached or remote. Michael Jones also makes the point that some men like the count could be reckless beyond reason and fight in seemingly hopeless positions, while others, however, would simply either run off or refuse to fight. He also reminds the reader that medieval battle was not a continuous event:

> The mêlée – the clash of dismounted men-at-arms – bore all the characteristics of a heavy weight slugging match. This could become so exhausting that both sides would briefly halt, before continuing again. This may seem an astonishing concept to us, imagining men, in the midst of beating the brains out of their opponents, stopping to take a time-out before resuming a frenzy of killing. Yet in some battles it actually happened by mutual agreement, the break being marked by a chosen signal. This was not an indicator of treachery, anymore than half-time in a sports fixture might be. At the Battle of Neville's

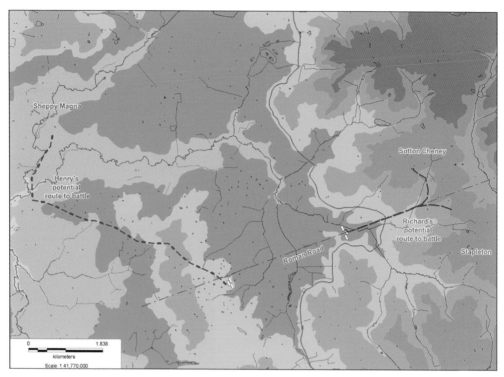

A map of Richard's and Henry's potential routes into battle.

Cross in 1346 English and Scottish foot soldiers set at each other in full-blooded combat. Once, if not twice, the exhausted troops on both sides lay down their weapons and took a brief respite. The struggle then resumed in all its intensity. As one contemporary put it, both sides 'rested by agreement and then fought on'.

What must be remembered by the modern reader is that any accounts by the winning side might imply that one side (the winners) were making a positive tactical re-grouping of their forces, while the enemy was showing a lack of will to fight or even signs of treachery to their leader. In reality, both sides were simply having to stop from sheer exhaustion.

Chapter 6

The Opening Salvoes

Conventionally, medieval battles would have started as early as possible in the morning. This was not to allow it to run on for 8 or 10 hours before nightfall, but to provide the combatants with the opportunity of fighting in the cool of the day. The biggest killer in a medieval battle was dehydration.

My interpretation of the battle finds that have been found so far is that the Duke of Norfolk led Richard's right battalion out from the safety of the track immediately to the north of Fenn Lane. He may have mounted the rise, deliberately showing himself to his enemy before moving off in a slow north-

A French fleur-de-lis horse pendant found close to the possible route of Norfolk's troops.

westerly arc, passing just to the south of the small village of Shenton with the intention of either attacking or at least drawing out Henry's left flank, which was under the control of Tudor's leading commander, the Earl of Oxford. As soon as Norfolk saw Oxford moving his men out to defend his master's flank, Norfolk took the deliberate action of moving still further north. This was not an attempt to out-flank Oxford, but a premeditated ploy to drag him as far away from Henry as possible. The *Crowland Chronicle* tells us that Henry had before the start of the battle given Oxford command of his French soldiers.

Today a public footpath follows the line of a water course (the River Anker) out in a north-westerly direction. Was this the line of an old trackway that Norfolk used? There have certainly been a number of archaeological finds along the route, including horse pendants. The move would also explain the point, so often quoted by modern historians, made by the original Tudor court historian, Polydore Vergil, in *Urbinatis Anglicæ Historiæ Libri Vigintiseptem*, who in turn had gleaned it from the actual men who had fought for Henry:

There was a marsh between them, which Henry deliberately left on his right, to serve his men as a defensive wall. In doing this he simultaneously *put the sun behind him*. The king, as soon as he saw the enemy advance past the marsh, ordered his men to charge. Suddenly raising a great shout they attacked first with arrows, and their opponents, in no wise holding back from the fight, returned the fire fiercely. When it came to close quarters, however, the dealing was done with swords.

There are certainly even to this day areas within many of the fields to the north of Fenn Lane that lie extremely wet – even in summer. However, little if any specific work has been done to ascertain whether these areas were wet – or more specifically 'marsh' – in 1485.

A marsh, be it a current one or one that has dried out due either to a natural change in the water table or modern drainage, will have a certain underlying geology. That is one with alluvium deposits. Alluvium is a general term for clay, silt, sand, gravel or similar unconsolidated detrital material, deposited during comparatively recent geologic time by a stream or other body of running water as a sorted or semi-sorted sediment. These deposits can be seen on geological maps, and it is only in these areas that a marsh could be located. However, a marsh that was present during the late medieval period (i.e. during the time of the battle) could not have any evidence of medieval ridge and furrow. The map below shows the known alluvium deposits with the ridge and furrow plotted by Peter Hall for the 2005–8 Battlefield Research Project.

A map showing the ridge and furrow (brown) and alluvium (yellow) deposits in the area of the Fenn Lane.

The marsh at Bosworth must have been sizeable enough for the early accounts to mention it as a feature in the landscape, but, using a Sherlock Holmes analogy again, it was not like the bogs described in *The Hound of the Baskervilles* where as soon as one stepped off the path, you were up to your neck in mud.

I suspect that here the local serf could drive his one cow from his hovel to market and keep his feet dry. However, a 'foreign' lord and his retinue of armed men would avoid it to ensure that they were able to keep together as an effective fighting force. A more in-depth, intensive survey needs to be carried out to plot the true expanse of all the medieval marsh areas and exactly where within the alluvium deposits these marshy sites were.

Either way, Oxford moving out towards Norfolk could well have marched towards these areas before turning in a northerly direction causing at least a marsh to be on his right flank.

Another case of 'There was a marsh between them, which Henry deliberately left on his right' should in fact read 'There was a marsh between them, which Henry's *men/leading commander* deliberately left on his right.'

Mike Ingram, in his book *Richard III and the Battle of Bosworth*, positions the main two protagonists at 90 degrees to the road. He bases this in part on the direction of the ridge and furrow. Mike suggests that the armies would (indeed could) only have fought up and down the ridge and furrow, and not across them:

> Surviving ridges are parallel, ranging from three to 22 yards (three to 20m) apart and up to 24 inches (61cm) tall – but could be up to six feet high (182cm) in places. Research on three battlefields of Northamptonshire (Edgcote, Northampton and Naseby) by Northamptonshire Battlefields Society and the Nasby Battlefields Project suggests that battles all took place along the line of the ridge and furrow and not across it. Trying to cross them would have constituted a considerable obstacle and horses would have likely refused.

He goes on to state:

> At Bosworth, the ridge and furrow is, for the most part, 90 degrees to Fenn Lane, including down from the ridge. A separate strip also leads from the battlefield on to Crown Hill. Their identification, therefore, points to the direction of troop movements.

What is not made clear – and potentially more important than 'just' the ridge and furrow at Edgcote, Northampton and Naseby – is where were any roads within their landscapes. I would suggest that an army (especially dragging heavy ordnance to a battle) would always choose to use the easier route of road rather than fields. If a road ran in parallel to the ridge and furrow, then obviously an army might expect to choose to run with the ridge. However, if, as with Bosworth, some of the road runs 'across' the ridge and furrow I would certainly expect an army might choose to move with the road, and against the ridge and furrow – depending most importantly where the enemy was positioned within the landscape.

With the Bosworth scenario, as with so many other things to do with Bosworth, there could be another reason why the two main armies chose to fight across the ridge and furrow.

There would have most likely been standing wheat or barley on the ridges 136 years before the armies met on that fateful August morning in 1485. However, almost overnight, those crops would have died where they stood simply because there would not have been enough people to gather them in. Plague had arrived. Millions of people were dying.

The area of ground we know today from the archaeological evidence as at least part of the battle site falls at the extremes of four parishes – Dadlington, Stoke Golding, Upton and Shenton. If half of the people in your village had died, why would you drag your ox and plough to the extreme edge of the parish when you had land closer? More importantly, if that land was only of marginal quality, you simply would not bother.

That ground would quickly pass from arable to pasture. Not only that but over 135 years one could imagine that the ridges would have been eroded and the furrows would have started to backfill. It would not be unimaginable that the ground by 1485 was more undulating than heavily ridge and furrow. Any half-decently trained war horse would have been able to cross wherever his rider wanted, and in whatever direction he needed to go.

Before 2009, people assumed that the battle would have commenced with a lot of jeering troops slowly marching towards each other, until they got to within 250m of each other. At this distance the archers, so feared by European armies, would have moved to the front and drawn their bows back to full draw, and then loosed their iron-tipped arrows towards the enemy. It was the medieval equivalent of carpet-bombing – indiscriminate and not overly effective. This opening volley would have been quickly followed by one side or other charging forward to start hand-to-hand combat.

Though we have found no evidence of the undoubted arrow storms (because we have not yet actively searched for iron arrow heads), what has been discovered, with the help of the dedicated work of the metal-detecting team, has caused us to rethink what happened in those few decisive minutes between Oxford and Norfolk. What we were not expecting to find, but ultimately have done, was a number of roundshot. These relatively small lead and lead-composite spheres most probably preceded the initial volley of arrows. What we do not yet know is where the guns

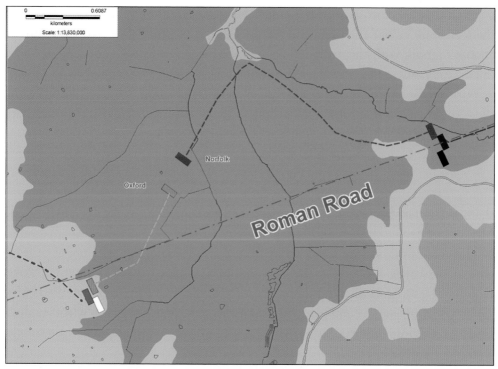

Map showing the positions of Norfolk and Oxford as they engaged at the opening of the battle.

Map showing all roundshot found in the area of the potential Oxford/Norfolk clash.

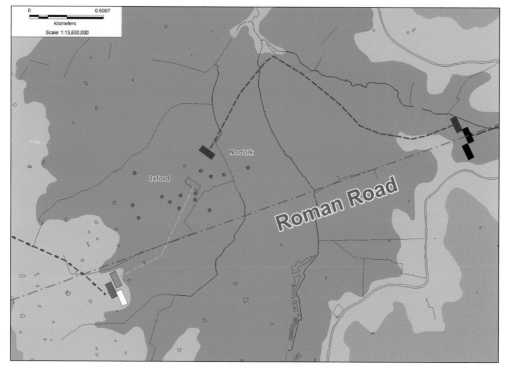

that fired them were positioned. What we can say though, is that the gunners must have been able to see the enemy, as they did not have the technology to fire over the horizon into an unseen enemy.

Our modern reproduction firing has managed to send replica lead spheres up to 1,200m when fired in a flat and horizontal barrel position. These tests were carried out over ground very close to the true site of the battle and on similar soil, but across short stubble. The roundshot were visually tracked and subsequently plotted on a map. It was found that though the shot travelled a complete distance of approximately 1,200m, it bounced every 50m or so across the field, until rolling to a final stop. The question must be, would a medieval gunner fire his cannon when only in the 'level' position? Some argue that this is all they would do. However, I would suggest that if one looks at the contemporary illustrations of early medieval field cannon, the gunners had the technology to elevate the barrel. If you can elevate the barrel, you likely can gain extra distance.

With a longbow an archer reaches maximum distance when the bow is at an elevation of 42 degrees. The arrow leaves the bow and arcs high over a distance until coming down to earth and (if it misses its target) sticks in the ground. It will only ever hit one target. With roundshot you want to play skittles with the enemy. You want to bounce it into the ranks of men in front of you. You do not want to drop a ball onto the head of only one of your enemy. You want to cut a swathe

A contemporary illustration of a sixteenth-century field gun, showing that these were not always fired 'flat and level'.

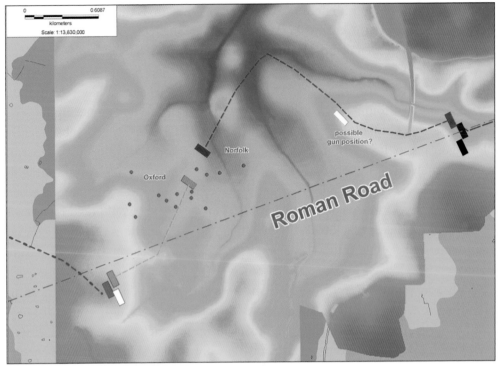

Map showing the possible position of 'Norfolk's Gun'.

through the ranks of those advancing troops. Therefore, you do not want to fire at maximum elevation, but I suggest an elevation increase of say 10 degrees would mean that your range might increase to over 1,500m. You do not need your shot first bouncing at 50m, as your enemy is hopefully still 500m away.

When you look at original cannon, the engineering is there in the gun to change its elevation. If every gunner were only ever to shoot 'flat and level', why would someone spend all that time and skill in making a gun move within

A roundshot from the battlefield (in the hand of the author), seen for the first time in nearly 525 years.

its frame, if not to give it elevation? The topography of the battle site is therefore critical. The difference in the lay of land between you and your enemy could be the difference between you hitting him with roundshot, or the enemy being able to overrun you as your shot hits rising ground or sinks into mud, short of the target.

Chapter 7

The Death of Norfolk

T he Duke of Norfolk would have followed up his initial attack from bow and cannon with hand-to-hand fighting. However, small lead shot have also been found in the area suggesting that not only were people in the melee fighting with sword and bill, but also with hand gun.

According to both Polydore Vergil and Jean Molinet, another near contemporary source, Norfolk engaged with Oxford's smaller force in vicious hand-to-hand fighting. To try and avoid being crushed in that first onslaught by superior forces, Oxford made his troops stand in a triangular, or wedge, formation, which caused confusion and communication breakdowns within Norfolk's ranks. As with many medieval leaders, Norfolk would have thrown himself into the thickest fighting. He was probably fighting on foot against other knights and

An early medieval handgunner.

men-at-arms until he was mortally wounded. Against all the odds Oxford was holding his own against the greater numbers and may have even been pushing Norfolk's men back.

We are told in the 'Song of Lady Bessy' – a near contemporary poem written for Thomas Stanley, that Norfolk himself died by a mill. With help from local landowners, we have been able to identify a field that has been known by the family as Mill Field for generations. When the detecting team searched this field, located just within the parish of Dadlington, a number of high-status items were discovered. Among the finds were a spur rowel, a gold finger ring and a silver gilded heraldic badge. All these finds are undoubtedly from the battle. The question is, are they from the site of Norfolk's last stand or even his death?

A gold finger ring, missing its fitting.

There have been many stories over the years about who fought or who was present at the Battle of Bosworth, including at least one about one of the 'Nephews in the Tower' who was reportedly living in France after 1485. This was probably a story started by someone trying to put a case forward for showing that Richard could not have had them killed. A second story

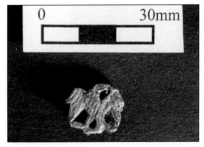

A silver heraldic badge.

was that one of Richard III's bastard sons was brought to the battle camp on the eve of the battle, and subsequently saw his father killed the following day. Today these stories are mostly dismissed as unlikely.

In 2016 Professor Shurer researched the heraldic badge seen above, of the 'bird facing right with open wings'. He is convinced he can put a name to it – and if he is right, and I certainly think he is, we have a new twist to 'The Bosworth Tale'. To have your heraldic device made from silver and gilded would most likely mean you were also a person of high standing (and your father probably of even higher standing). In heraldry, the way to signify a recognised person but of illegitimate birth (a bastard son) was to turn the heraldic device to look the 'wrong way'. Could the father of the person wealthy enough to have gilded silver buttons have been a king?

One plausible explanation would be one of the two people thought to be bastard sons of Richard III for they could also claim a high-standing, royal link. John of Gloucester was knighted at York on 8 September 1483 during the investiture of his half-brother Edward of Middleham as Prince of Wales. He was appointed Captain of Calais by his father on 11 March 1485, and in the letter of appointment Richard refers to John as 'our dear bastard son'.

Richard of Eastwell, a bricklayer of Eastwell, near Ashford in Kent, made claims to be a natural son of Richard III. He was said to have been brought up without knowing the identity of his parents but was boarded with a schoolmaster who taught him Latin, a sign of someone being educated according to his status. He was visited four times a year by a mysterious gentleman who paid for his upkeep. He also claimed that when still a young child he was taken to his father's tent on the night before the Battle of Bosworth in 1485, and King Richard informed the boy that he was his son and told him to watch the battle from a safe vantage point. The king further told the boy that if he won he would acknowledge him as his son. If he lost he told the boy to forever conceal his identity.

Professor Shurer has however identified the owner of this small, but potentially massively significant find. The owner was indeed a bastard – not of Richard, but of Edward IV.

The 'Nephews in the Tower' were two of ten children of Edward IV and may well have been dead. Another of Edward's known children was Arthur Plantagenet. He was born sometime before 1472 and died in 1542. He was known to have been a soldier, diplomat and administrator.

The identity of Arthur's mother and his date of birth have given rise to much speculation. The editor of his correspondence, Muriel St Clare Byrne, agrees with most authorities in identifying his mother as Elizabeth Lucy, an obscure lady who was probably the daughter of Thomas Waite of Hampshire. However, Ashdown-Hill, in his book *The Mythology of the 'Princes in the Tower'* (2018), disputes this. Stories that Arthur's mother was Elizabeth (Jane) Shore or Lady Eleanor Butler can be discounted. Byrne suggests a date of birth between 1462 and 1464, but this seems unlikely for two reasons. First, it presupposes that Edward IV did not beget, or at any rate acknowledge, any illegitimate children after his marriage to Elizabeth Woodville in 1465. Second, a 50-year-old uncle seems an unlikely jousting companion for the young Henry VIII in the early 1510s.

The first possible reference to Arthur occurs in 1472 when 'my Lord the Bastard' is mentioned in the accounts of the royal household. This scrap suggests that Arthur may have been brought up in the royal nursery alongside Edward IV's legitimate children, who were born between 1466 and 1480. Although Byrne contends that Arthur probably spent much of his childhood with his mother's family in Hampshire, it is likely that this proximity to the royal family continued into Henry VII's reign. His early life is obscured, however, by the lack of contemporary references to him. In 1501 he was probably 'the Bastard of King Edward's' whom Henry VII recommended to his mother. By the following year, if not before, he had entered the household of his half-sister, Queen Elizabeth of York, and was listed among her household servants at her funeral in 1503. As such he was probably known to the young Prince Henry, the future Henry VIII, who was brought up in the royal nursery at Eltham Palace under the guidance of the queen's household staff. After the queen's death he was transferred to the king's household, serving as an esquire for the body. In April 1509 he made the transition to Henry VIII's household.

It is evident that in the first years of Henry VIII's reign Arthur Plantagenet was a close companion of the young king. In May and June 1510, along with such intimates of the king as Charles Brandon, Edmund Howard and Thomas Knyvet, he took part in feats of arms at court. He participated in the campaigns of 1513, initially at sea, when he nearly lost his life in the shipwreck of the *Nicholas of Hampton* in February, and later in the king's invasion of France during the summer; he was dubbed a knight outside Tournai on 14 October 1513.

Arthur Plantagenet, 1st Viscount Lisle was therefore not only the bastard son of Edward IV, and the nephew of Richard III, but he was the half-brother of Queen Elizabeth of York (and therefore the brother-in-law to Henry VII) and thus an uncle of King Henry VIII. It also seems that he may well have been at Bosworth – but did he fight on the side of King Richard? Probably not, as he is not mentioned in any known accounts and would have been between 13 and 19 years of age.

However, it seems he may possibly have been present at the battle, but purely as an observer. Perhaps he stood behind Richard's guns in the lea of that raising ground where the Ricardian troops had formed up into their three battalia at the start of the battle and where Norfolk was brought back to have his wounds checked by the barber-surgeon.

It is not such a leap of imagination to assume that the two nobles, undoubtedly known to each other, even with an age gap of about forty-five years, would wish to speak to each other before one passed away having potentially suffered horrendous injuries that both probably knew were going to be fatal. Did Arthur take off his expensive doublet and put it under Norfolk's head for him to rest on, losing a button in the process? Could the ring found nearby also have belonged to him? Unfortunately, due to the fact no insert, stone or gem, has been found, with or without a heraldic device, we will probably never know.

To add weight to the suggestion that Norfolk moved out and back along the line of the present public footpath, the landowners 'have always' called a field running adjacent to this route the 'Battle Field'. If indeed there had been a clash between Oxford and Norfolk in this immediate area, some of the dead at least may have been buried near where they fell, placed in a natural hollow, adjacent to a stream feeding the Anker. If this grave pit could be located today, we may be able to learn more of this clash. This might include how some of them met their end. Was it by arrow, halberd or 'small gonne' fire?

We may, in fact, already have a clue as to where to start looking. During the work carried out between 2005 and 2010, Peter Masters of Cranfield University was asked to come to Bosworth and undertake some investigations. His area of specialism is geophysics, which can be used to create maps of any subsurface features that contrast with their surroundings, such as old ditches or remains of walls or foundations. In some cases, individual objects can also be detected as well as old water courses.

Masters was asked to carry out four surveys. One just to the south of the Fenn Lane, to see if any evidence for the line of the Roman road and potential ford could be picked up. While the second site was about 800m to the north of the lane, and was deliberately chosen to try and find any remains of a grave pit. The following is an extract from Masters's final report, the *Geophysical Survey at Bosworth Battlefield, Shenton, Leicestershire*:

Field 3 was surveyed to locate the remains of an alleged mass grave. The survey area covered 2ha of ground. Two linear anomalies were detected, the southernmost one with two large oak trees still standing along its alignment, denote the remains of former field boundaries as depicted on the first edition Ordnance Survey map of 1885. The northern field boundary shows a discrete group of dipolar anomalies indicating modern ferrous activity possibly caused by the removal of the former hedge line. A linear dipolar anomaly runs parallel to the eastern hedge boundary indicating the presence of a service trench. At the northern end of this service trench, a discrete amorphous zone indicating modern ferrous disturbance denotes the remains of a former barn as depicted on the first edition Ordnance Survey map of 1885. The service may have once been connected to the building. A series of discrete individual anomalies can be seen across the entire image. These indicate iron spikes possibly representing ferrous remains such as horseshoes, stray iron fragments and other ferrous objects. A series of ephemeral curvilinear anomalies were detected on the western side of the field close to the gate and footpath entrance. These are likely to represent animal tracks created by sheep or where people have been constantly walking. They do not appear to indicate features of archaeological interest due to their faint nature. No further significant anomalies were detected.

Therefore, unfortunately, no grave pit was found during this particular survey. However, the reason for looking in the first place was based on local information. After that survey was carried out more details were received from a local resident who, as a young boy during the war, remembered a group of navvies digging ditches on Shenton Estate. They were digging in the field adjacent to Shenton Lane when they 'came across a number of skeletons, all of which had suffered horrendous injuries'. The informant went on to say that because the war was not going well at that time, it was 'decided that it would be best to re-cover the pit and leave things well alone'. However, the lad was quick enough to note where the pit was, and using a couple of gateways and a tree as references, he recorded the location in his diary. About seventy odd years later I have superimposed both the Cranfield survey data and the local suggested site for the alleged mass grave. As can be seen in the map on the following page, they are frustratingly close to each other.

In an order of 19 February 1484 King Richard III gave funds to two churches so that the bodies from the earlier Battle of Towton in 1461 could be reburied in consecrated ground. The wording of this order is quite specific, not least because it fits with the limited archaeological evidence so far to date. That being existing pits or hollows had been used for the initial burial, and that these bodies were not moved to an existing burial site. The same technique seems to have been used at Bosworth.

Vergil suggests that after the battle Henry Tudor went up a nearby hill, and after thanking his men, 'ordered the wounded to be tended, and the dead to be buried'.

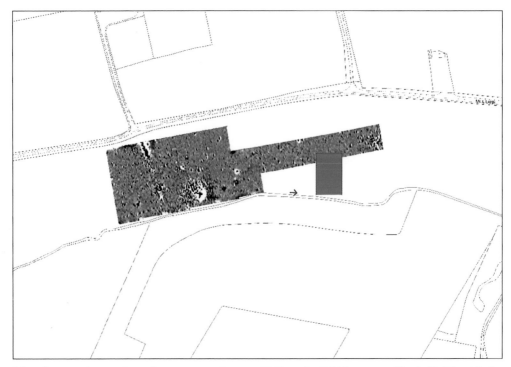

Map showing the geophysical survey carried out in 2008 in the field known as 'Battle Field', with the area later identified as a possible burial pit marked in red.

Most academics believe that at some point the bodies were subsequently moved to the church at Dadlington. This must have happened within twenty-five years of the original battle, as by August 1511, as a text of an indulgence to be given to those who contributed money states, the chapel was the place 'to which bodies or bones of the men slain in Bosworth field have been brought'. The reference to bones suggests that there must have been at least some exhumation from the actual battlefield and the original grave pits for a more final and fitting reburial. For many years there have been numerous undocumented finds of skulls and disarticulated bones in and around Dadlington churchyard. However, presumably only those pits that were still known about could be exhumed. Is the one in 'Battle Field' one that the locals had forgotten about?

Chapter 8

Preparing to Charge

I n *The Tragedy of Richard III*, 1.1.14–31, William Shakespeare describes Richard in such a way as to make him appear as the evil opposite of Henry's spotless character:

> I, that am curtail'd of this fair proportion, cheated of feature by dissembling nature, deform'd, unfinish'd, sent before my time into this breathing world, scarce half made up, and that so lamely and unfashionable That dogs bark at me as I halt by them; why, I, in this week piping time of peace, have no delight to pass away the time, Unless to spy my shadow in the sun and descant on mine own deformity. And therefore, since I cannot prove a lover, to entertain theses fair well-spoken days, I am determined to prove a villain and hate the idle pleasures of these days.

However, Polydore Vergil, Henry Tudor's official historian, tells us that '... King Richard, alone was killed fighting manfully in the thickest press of his enemies'.

Today we know that by the time of his death, Richard suffered from a physical condition. That of adolescent-onset scoliosis. However, what is harder to determine is how debilitating this was for Richard. How effective was Richard in a medieval battle?

We know that Edward IV appointed Richard the sole Commissioner of Array for the Western Counties in 1464, when he was 11. By the age of 17 he had an independent command. He fought, as the Duke of Gloucester, at the battles of Barnet (possibly leading Edward's vanguard) and at Tewkesbury in 1471 while still an 18-year-old. Richard led the English forces that recaptured Berwick-upon-Tweed from the Kingdom of Scotland in 1482. However, how much actual fighting he undertook during this campaign is sketchy.

How could the 'hunchback king' be such a formidable warrior? For this suggests that his scoliosis did not apparently impair him to any great extent, or at least not in his early life. Now we have a far better idea, thanks to a young man from Tamworth, in Staffordshire, called Dominic Smee.

Scoliosis is an abnormal curvature of the spine. The normal spine has gentle natural curves that round the shoulders and make the lower back curve inward. Scoliosis typically causes issues with the spinal column and rib cage. The spine curves from side to side at varying degrees, and some of the spinal bones may rotate slightly, making the hips or shoulders appear uneven. Today scoliosis affects about 2–3 per cent of the population. It can occur in adults but is more commonly diagnosed for the first time in children between 10 and 15 years of age. About 10 per cent of adolescents have some degree of scoliosis, but less than 1 per cent of them develop scoliosis that requires treatment. The condition also tends to run in families. Among persons with relatives who have scoliosis, about 20 per cent develop the condition.

Patients with severe conditions, particularly those with underlying neuromuscular disorders, may possibly develop what is called restrictive thoracic disease. This term refers to problems with breathing and, at times, trouble obtaining enough oxygen, due to a smaller chest cavity. This smaller chest cavity results from the original deformities, or sometimes just from any subsequent surgery. The resulting restricted chest cavity is also less able to expand when breathing.

Dominic Smee has the same rare form of adolescent-onset scoliosis that Richard III had, resulting in spinal curvature of approximately 75 degrees to the right along with an S-shaped curvature of the ribs. In 2014, Dominic volunteered to take part in a series of challenges with the help of several experts. This even included a cavalry charge, to assess what the king might have been capable of when he went into battle. Dominic went on to prove that Richard III's scoliosis need not have prevented him from fulfilling his role as a warrior. 'With my scoliosis, you might think I was a bit stooped, but you wouldn't really see there was a problem unless I was undressed,' Dominic says. 'With Richard III, it's looking like the same story. Far from being a hunchback, he would have looked pretty normal in a suit of armour. He'd just have had to have armour specially made.' But then I would add, what wealthy nobleman, let alone a king, would not have his armour made to measure?

Dominic was fitted for a bespoke 30kg, £25,000 harness, otherwise commonly called a suit of armour, for a Channel 4 documentary – *Richard III 'The New Evidence'*, broadcast in 2014. He was also taught to ride, and in the documentary he is seen recreating the king's cavalry charge at Bosworth. He also found that, rather than hindering him, the armour actually provided support, strengthening his upper body. The medieval saddle, with its rigid construction and stiff back, provided additional support. Having previously given up on sporting activities in his teens, finding them 'degrading and demoralising', Dominic described the cavalry charge as 'exhilarating'.

This might imply that because of his scoliosis Richard could really only fight on horseback as, on foot, especially with relatively heavy armour on and a restrictive, full-face helmet which he undoubtedly wore, his breathing would have been

A knight on horseback showing a saddle with a high pommel and cantle.

probably impeded. Therefore, his *mounted* charge was inevitable. Once he was on foot his *defeat* was equally inevitable.

I also believe that Richard was an experienced tactician. He would have spent some time, probably on the Sunday evening, with his commanders planning what he wanted everyone to do. His master plan was to try and open up the battlefield as much as possible. Norfolk was to pull Oxford away from Tudor as much as possible. He needed Tudor exposed, so that Richard could then lead a mounted charge against this man who was calling himself 'The Rightful King'. More importantly, the battle needed to be over, and before a third army led by the Stanleys could possibly intervene.

Here we have another question. Who actually made up this 'third army'? Or indeed was there a fourth? The Stanley brothers, Thomas, Lord Stanley and Sir William Stanley, were from an immensely powerful family, owning huge amounts of land in the north of England. They were also smart political figures. Their support was critical, in terms of men and loyalty to both Richard and Henry.

Thomas, Lord Stanley had been a steward in Edward IV's (Richard's brother) household, as well as Constable of England under Richard III. However, he was also married to Henry Tudor's mother, Margaret Beaufort, and there was the very real danger that the Stanleys would desert the king, especially when Lord Stanley excused himself on the pretext of illness.

Most academics usually put both Sir William Stanley and his brother Thomas, Lord Stanley *at* the Battle with two armies. Some even go as far as to suggest that not only did both brothers bring their own armies, but they placed them in *different* positions within the landscape, one north, one south. Even contemporary sources cannot agree. We are led to believe by Vergil that 'the Stanleyans, whereof about 3,000 were at the battle, under the conduct of William'. He puts 'Lord Stanley' halfway between the armies which makes Henry nervous. The 'Ballad of Bosworth Field' also puts 'Lord Stanley' on a 'hill' and this threat to Richard causes the order to be given to execute Lord Strange (Lord Stanley's son, whom Richard was holding hostage). The *Crowland Chronicle* puts them both on the field. Interestingly we are also told in rediscovered papers, 'Vatican Regesta 685: 1484–1487', *Calendar of Papal Registers Relating to Great Britain and Ireland*, Vol. 14: 1484–1492 (1960), pp. 14–30, that:

> Thomas, earl of Derby, and lord de Stanlley [*sic*], fifty years of age, sworn, etc., and diligently examined of and about the above schedule and its contents. And first, of and about his knowledge of the persons of the aforesaid king and lady, says that he has known the aforesaid king well since the 24th day of August, (fn. 11) and the said lady for fifteen years.

In other words, Thomas, Lord Stanley, did not *meet* Henry until two days after the battle, and therefore one would surmise that the implication is that he therefore was not at the battle.

It is also important to understand that consideration must be given to the family's need to survive. Their self-interest had already seen a simple but effective insurance policy, in which the family tried to back both sides in a conflict. For example, at Blore Heath in 1459, Sir William was sent to one side while Lord Stanley remained close to their opponents, promising support, but finding countless excuses to not actually finally commit. It is not implausible that a similar strategy was followed at Bosworth and, if this was the case, and Lord Stanley did not join the fighting (or was not even present), the hostage taking may have worked. Richard had no need to execute his captive.

Whichever of the Stanleys was present, most sources imply that their men were positioned somewhere between the armies of Henry in the east and Richard in the west and on high ground overlooking the centre field, where the fighting was about to take place. If my general interpretation of the finds to the north of Fenn Lane is correct (and they must surely be, as we know Norfolk was on Richard's right flank and Oxford was on Henry's left), then Stanley could only be to the south of the two opposing armies, on the high ground to the east of the village of Stoke Golding.

I would suggest that for Richard's plan to work not only was it easier to have Oxford out of the way, in the north of the battle area (hence Norfolk drawing him out, and away from Henry), but Richard himself would have to get within striking range of Henry before Sir William intervened. To do this, both Richard's battle and Northumberland's moved east, towards Henry. I think they drew themselves up into two battles, on the slightly rising ground some 1,400m to the east of Henry and Talbot (who led Henry's right battle). If this is the case, Stanley would have been seen as a direct threat to Richard. To counter that threat, I suggest that Northumberland would have turned his troops to look south-west and directly facing Stanley, as a counter-measure to any potential assault. At 1,400m Richard's and Northumberland's guns would be close enough to engage the enemy, and this is what I think they must have done.

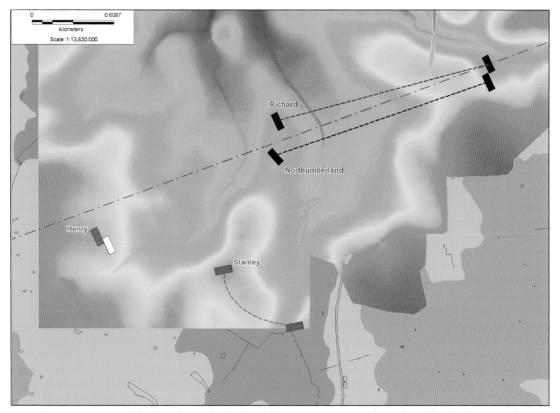

A map showing Richard and Northumberland have moved east, while William Stanley has moved to overlook the two opposing armies. Henry is static.

By 2015 we had found eighteen roundshot, scattered over an area of approximately 0.75sq km. What we do not know is, was it all fired from Richard's guns? In the Parliamentary Record of November 1485, it states that 'Richard of Gloucester brought all manner of arms' to the field including 'guns, bows, arrows, spears (etc.)' when he 'traitorously levied war against our sovereign lord'. What we are not told is whether Henry did (or did not) bring gun as well. One can assume in this 'Act of Attainder' against Richard, who at the time of the battle was the anointed king, that the truth may have been somewhat stretched.

What better piece of spin-doctoring after the battle than to talk about that evil Richard, not only bringing twice as many men to the battle but gun as well. Yet, Henry, by the grace of God, still won! At no time is this a lie. Indeed, Philip de Commynes, who was a writer and diplomat in the courts of Burgundy and France, wrote five years after the battle in 1490 that the king of France assisted Henry in his preparations for invading England. This included 'some artillery'. Indeed, the thirty-fifth roundshot that were found at Sheepy would actually suggest that Henry *did* indeed have gun with him. He could easily have gathered them from either Lichfield or Tamworth or indeed even Atherstone. He may even have brought them all the way from France. More interestingly, potentially, is did Sir William also bring gun to the field? If so, did he use them in anger or simply show them off to both armies, taunting them with his military strength?

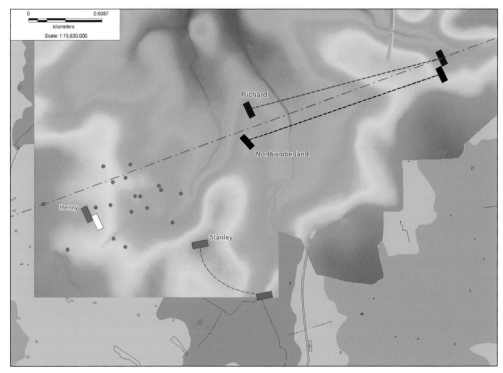

Map showing the roundshot scatter found around the assumed position of Henry.

Chapter 9

Richard's Charge – Stanley's Opportunity

H aving presumably at least intimidated the troops of Henry Tudor, if not softened them up, Richard then followed up his roundshot onslaught and attack on the enemy vanguard with what was, in my opinion, a clearly premeditated charge. It was not a knee-jerk reaction to Sir William Stanley's presence, let alone the fear of Northumberland's potential treachery, as some people have suggested.

To undertake anything resembling a mounted charge (which everyone agrees did happen) Richard must have had his knights with him, and prepared to undertake that manoeuvre. A medieval charge was a mass of men and horse, all in plate, crossing the landscape in a close, controlled block. Knight would ride knee to knee with his adjacent knight in a solid wall of steel. The manoeuvre would start with the destriers, or medieval warhorses, walking forward. This would be followed by them moving up to a controlled canter, until the last minute when, and only then, they would be spurred on into a headlong gallop. The average speeds covered by a horse are as follows:

At a walk, 6.4km/hour – 4 miles/hour
At a trot, about 10km/hour – 6¼ miles/hour
At a slow canter, about 20km/hour – 12½ miles/hour
At a gallop, about 40km/hour – 25 miles/hour

A fifteenth-century cavalry block has two main advantages. The first is mobility, the second is speed, combined with full armour and high-impact weaponry it is a fearful and potentially highly effective weapon. The normal reaction to seeing enemy cavalry on the horizon must be for the sensible military leader to adjust his troop position to defend against a possible charge. This may mean he has to re-form his infantry, turning his troops to face full frontal against the cavalry, or sending his own cavalry to intercept. It is a misconception that defending against cavalry was not a problem for arrows and fixed poles. This notion first requires that your infantry be facing the correct way, and secondly that they have 'the bottle' to stand their ground against a wall of thundering steel coming towards them.

Today it is very difficult to imagine what went through the mind of the mounted knight charging into battle, let alone the man on the receiving end of such an onslaught, many of whom probably had never been in battle before, standing there with little physical protection, let alone training. However, I have discussed the role of fifteenth-century cavalry with members of Destrier, a modern group of horsemen who in 2008 became instrumental in pushing the boundaries of recreating the medieval tournament, and who are rightly acknowledged as pioneers of modern jousting. They became the first men (and women) in modern history to ride horses in heavy jousting harnesses while breaking real lances upon each other.

Jousting is obviously nothing like a medieval battle. However, members of the group participated in a two-day event in Bexbach, Germany, where they spent a full 48 hours working as a cavalry unit against infantry and artillery in an open battle scenario across several hectares of landscape. This resulted in several key experiences confirming a lot of assumed medieval tactical theory. It was found, for example, that it was often best for the mounted units to ride around the enemy position out of sight, and then make themselves visible, watch the enemy unit scramble and once, suitably re-deployed, simply disappear again behind the hill or into the woods from whence they had come. Quarter of an hour later they would turn up again, this time on the opposite side of the enemy, causing them to have to rearrange themselves yet again. Cavalry combining the impact of extremely dangerous fighting force with high mobility will shape enemy tactics as soon as it becomes visible. Therefore, any cavalry commander will attempt to keep his unit hidden for as long as possible, unless he deliberately wants to use that as a specific tactic.

How can we apply this knowledge to Bosworth? If, as I have already suggested, Richard and Norfolk's infantry have moved forward onto that small spit of slightly rising ground approximately 1,400m in front of Henry, where were Richard's mounted troops? The obvious position for the mounted men would be approximately halfway between Richard's now silent gun battery and his infantry, where they were probably out of sight of Henry's troops, but only 2,000m from them. This would mean that when Richard decided the time was right, he would have given the order for the charge to start. This would have been initially a walk or controlled trot forward over 500 or 600m, still out of sight of Henry's gaze. This walk or trot was important, for it would have allowed Richard's troops to make sure that they were together as an effective unit. To reach the rise in front of Henry would take somewhere between 3½ and 5½ minutes. Once that low, but so important, rise was reached, they would be in full view of Henry, their plan would have been exposed and Richard would have no time to waste. The mounted knights would now quicken their mounts on into a controlled canter. To cover the 1,400m to Henry, it would take Richard's mounted troops no more than 4 minutes. A total of less than 9½ minutes from start to finish.

Richard, of course, led from the front. He was King of England and it was his duty. He was also recreating his father's charge at the Battle of Wakefield in 1460. It was chivalrous to do so. For he was a warrior king. There was also a more practical reason. A cavalry charge is an exceedingly difficult beast to control. You have a large number of men with big egos, on even more powerful beasts, clad in full steel and with their visors down. There is minimal hearing, minimal sight and it is a struggle to turn their heads to check right or left. The only thing one can do in this position is follow the man in front. Consequently, the charge will go wherever the man in front goes. This is a principle that survives throughout the history of cavalry, even if not always successfully.

At Wakefield, Richard's father's charge was catastrophic. He died after leaving the high ground of Sandal Castle. His unexpected charge enabled his enemy to move in such a way that they drew his forces on and subsequently overwhelmed them. Eleven years later, Richard, himself then only 19, commanded his brother's vanguard at the Battle of Tewkesbury. Again, the enemy enticed them from the heights of a prepared defensive position. A more recent example can be seen in 1854, when Major General Cardigan led the Charge of the Light Brigade. Therefore, for Richard's charge to have any chance of success, he had to take the front position and lead it to *his* target.

We are told by Vergil that Richard first killed Sir William Brandon, Henry's banner bearer, before going on to unseat Sir John Cheney, 'a giant of a man'.

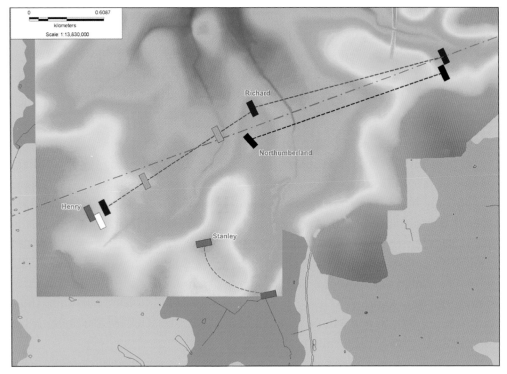

A map showing Richard's mounted assault on Henry's position.

However, he did not seem to reach Henry, who was possibly standing on foot behind his mounted knights or mercenary pikemen, as some suggest. The question one must ask is, did Richard not even aim for Henry? Cheney was there for one reason, and one alone – to give his life, if necessary, to defend his lord. That he did. However, I wonder if Richard deliberately targeted Brandon, who held the Tudor banner for all to see. Take down the banner and what quicker way to instil fear in the ranks of the mainly mercenary enemy? With the banner down, Tudor's troops might falter. Richard could always turn again, and attack Henry.

Andreas Wenzel, the chair of Destrier, summed this up brilliantly in 2016:

My personal view with regards to Richard's attack on Cheney and Brandon:

> Consider the above – visor down, restricted vision, virtually no hearing, you can't turn your head, a percentage of your concentration goes on controlling that mad stallion between your legs and the lance in your hand, and then all the adrenaline … you are not sitting in front of a targeting computer choosing rationally from a selection of available targets. Literally what happens in practice is this: A possible target turns up in your visor; you decide whether or not to engage; if you don't want to engage, you either need to move your horse's direction or go through that target. If I were Richard, I would have aimed my cavalry charge at the Tudor banner. As I would have come closer at speed, I don't think I would have had a lot of opportunity to figure out who all the other guys in armour are around the banner, and if one of them might possibly be Tudor. I would just try to take that banner down and then hope that the guys behind me will end up killing the right guy in armour. If a guy moves between me and the banner, I'd have to take him down so as not to change the direction of the charge (that would be Cheney).

Richard's plan, whatever it actually was, ultimately failed. Henry Tudor did not die in that initial charge and, having held off for a period of time, Sir William Stanley at last committed both himself and at least a percentage of his troops. Stanley only had to cover 1,000m to support Henry. At a canter he would have covered that distance in a little over 2 minutes from start to finish. Strategically placed between the two armies, and overlooking the mounted Richard, Stanley would have known exactly what Richard was attempting. He had 7 minutes to rally his mounted men and move them off to support Henry. He cut it fine but got there in time, not only to protect Henry, but to drive Richard right back into a marsh or mire, where, according to Molinet, Hall and Shakespeare, Richard lost not only his horse and his crown, but ultimately his life.

What could be seen as something of a more cynical view of Stanley might have been that if Richard had indeed killed Henry on that initial hit Stanley would have

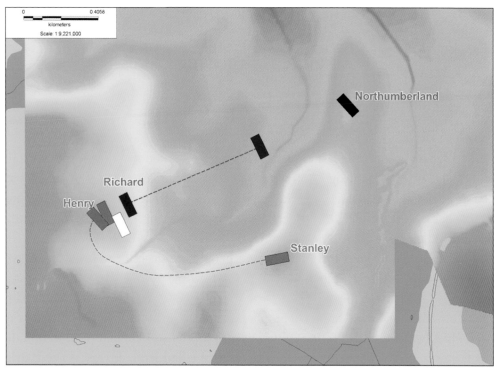

A map showing Stanley's move to support Henry Tudor, thus effectively ending the Battle of Bosworth.

been the first to cheer, saying, 'Well done, Sire; I waited for you to move and then I came to your support and tried to hit Henry in the rear. I made sure he could not retreat or run away like the Welsh Devil he was!' For the Stanleys always came out smelling of roses.

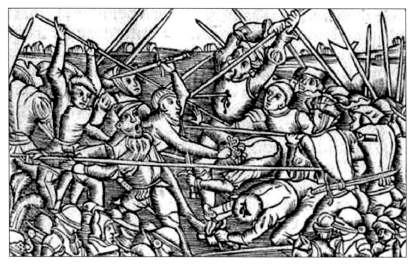

An unknow artist's impression of a close-quarter melee from a Renaissance martial arts treatise.

Chapter 10

The Death of Richard

Richard died in the last chivalric charge of mounted knights on British soil. He was the last English king to die in battle. Some academics describe it as a last, desperate bid of a madman in an attempt to keep the Crown. I do not think that is the case. As I have tried to suggest, it was a pre-planned and carefully executed manoeuvre that so nearly worked.

There are many times in history where people are described as daring, brave or even genius. There are also many times that people are described as desperate, foolhardy or reckless. Sometimes it can seem to be nothing more than a flip of a coin that makes a man fall into one category or the other. Richard was undoubtedly brave, the question is, was he also foolhardy? He had tried to imitate his father some twenty-five years before, when he had led a charge at the Battle of Wakefield. Some might say he copied him too closely, for his father also failed to win that day.

Do we know where Richard died? We are told in the *Chronicles* of Jean Molinet that Richard lost his horse in a marsh or mire, and Henry Tudor's proclamation states that he lost his life at a site called Sandeford. Logically Sandeford might be the place that the old Roman road crossed the marsh – the 'sandy ford'.

On a quiet September day in 2009, I was one of three metal-detectorists who were out in a field searching for evidence of the Battle of Bosworth. It had been an extremely unproductive couple of days until a small object was picked up by one of the team, Carl Dawson. The badge that he found was made of silver and gilded.

It is thought that this badge, now known as the 'Bosworth Boar', would have possibly been given by Richard himself to one of his very close, personal friends and supporters. It was found just on the edge of the only medieval marsh proven by scientists using carbon 14 dating techniques currently available. It was also close to the line of the old Roman road. Was this Sandeford?

The 'Bosworth Boar', found on 9 September 2009.

Do we know how Richard died? We know that Richard was a skilful soldier, and a feared enemy. We may never be able to prove where exactly he died, and until 2012 we would never have been able to say the injuries he received, which led to his death, but since finding his remains in Leicester we can at least confirm the injuries he received, which led to his death. Like most things to do with the Battle of Bosworth, this is, however, still open to interpretation.

After the excavation, the skeleton was taken to Leicester University where each individual bone was carefully cleaned. Once this delicate process had been carried out the experts, led by Dr Jo Appleby, observed more significant injuries than those first seen when the body was lying in the ground. At

Richard's memorial stone, now located in the battlefield heritage centre courtyard.

least eleven injuries can now be finally identified and are all certainly the result of wounds suffered either immediately before or immediately after death.

The injuries are:

1–3.   Three wounds to the left rear of the skull and the top of the skull.
4.   A small penetrating wound on top of the skull.
5.   A large hole underneath the back of the skull.
6.   A wound on the left base of the skull.
7.   A cut on the lower jaw.
8.   A hole in the right cheek.
9.   A tool mark on the right mandible.
10.   A cut on the right tenth rib.
11.   A cut on the inside of the pelvis.

1–3.   Three wounds to the left rear of the skull and the top of the skull – A sharp-bladed weapon has clipped the top-rear part of the skull three times, shaving off the top layer of bone, leaving a set of small circular depressions. On closer examination the experts were able to see striations caused by the blade on the bone. Further careful examination of those striations revealed that wound 1 and wound 2 share many similar characteristics and were therefore most likely caused by the same weapon, that weapon being a sword. It was not clear what weapon caused the third wound.

4. *A small penetrating wound on top of the skull* – This wound was caused by a sharp blow from a pointed weapon on the crown of the head. The weapon had enough force behind it to split the inside of the skull, leaving two small flaps of bone pushed inwards.

5. *A large hole underneath the back of the skull* – This is the single largest injury to the skull and is a hole where part of the base of the skull has been completely removed by a single slice. The experts all agree that this could have only been caused by a large, very sharp blade wielded with some force (and probably by someone with some skill). While it is not possible to prove which kind of weapon caused the injury, it is consistent with a halberd or something remarkably similar. An injury such as this would have been fatal.

6. *A wound on the left base of the skull* – A second injury to the base of the skull is a jagged hole in the lower left side of the skull. This is thought to have been carried out using a sword or similar bladed weapon which has cut through the bone. Closer examination of the interior of the skull revealed a mark opposite this wound, showing that the blade penetrated to a depth of 105mm. There is also a corresponding cut mark on the atlas vertebrae. An injury such as this would have been fatal.

7. *A cut on the lower jaw* – A blade has cut the right side of the chin.

8. *A hole in the right cheek* – This is a rectangular hole and may have been caused by a dagger or similar weapon piercing right through the cheek.

9. *A tool mark on the right mandible* – This mark consists of a number of fine striations which appear to have been caused by a sharp but unknown weapon.

10. *A cut on the right tenth rib* – This cut was caused by a sharp knife or dagger.

11. *A cut on the inside of the pelvis* – This was also produced by a sharp weapon such as a sword or dagger. The weapon was thrust from behind, entering the right buttock and penetrating right through the body.

As Richard would have been in plate armour during the battle, his torso would have been covered and therefore protected. Wound 10 therefore is thought most likely to represent a post-mortem injury, perhaps delivered as a 'punishment' or occurring in the act of cutting the armour and clothing as the body was stripped. Likewise, wound 11 would have been difficult to inflict during battle as again he would have been protected by his armour. The experts' assumption is therefore that this injury was also post-mortem and was possibly inflicted as an act of humiliation.

Looking at all eleven wounds, we can say that most likely at least two were post-mortem (10 and 11) and the other nine were received during the fighting. Of those nine, two (5 and 6) could have been the fatal wound. Can we take a guess at which one might be deemed to have been the first critical injury? For example, wound 8 could well have been made by the point of a dagger to the cheek when Richard was in the initial charge and subsequent melee and ultimately killing William Brandon, well before the final fight for his life. The wound would have smarted, but it was far from fatal, or even one that would have slowed Richard down. However, the wound that I think may well be the crucial (but not fatal) injury is wound 4.

Robert Woosnam-Savage, Curator at the Royal Armouries, was one of the few people who was part of both teams involved with the project. He was Project Weapons Expert for the University of Leicester 'Greyfriars Research' Team, as well as a member of the research team for the 'Looking for Richard Project' Team. He is one of the handful of experts to have physically examined the remains. He was employed to help find and examine the weapons trauma on the skeleton and attempt to identify the various types of weapons that may have been used to make them. He suggests that wound 4 was caused by a rondel dagger, as quoted in 'Perimortem trauma in King Richard III: a skeletal analysis', *The Lancet*:

> The shape of this injury is consistent with the stiff square-section blade often found on so-called rondel daggers. It is not consistent with other medieval weaponry. A war hammer would leave a larger injury, possibly with fractures, and a mace would probably leave marks from several of the flanges that made up the head of the weapon. An injury inflicted by a halberd or poleaxe top spike would probably have been delivered with greater force, and would have caused complete separation of the inner table flaps and, again, possible extensive fracturing. This injury might have been inflicted by a weapon that was the same as or similar to the one that gave rise to the injury on the right maxilla. The dimensions of the injury and the absence of any radiating fractures would also seemingly rule out an arrow strike.

Woosnam-Savage pre-empts this statement by suggesting that Richard by this time had no helmet on his head. Why would Richard, while still in the heat of battle, not have a helmet on? There are only two obvious reasons:

- As explained earlier, one possible side effect of severe scoliosis can be shortness of breath. If Richard was trying to fight on foot in full plate armour, he would more than likely be struggling to breath sufficiently to carry on fighting. The question is would an experienced combatant willingly take of his head protection during the thick of the battle?
- Someone got close enough to Richard to cut is chin strap and take his helmet off. (This might explain wounds 7, 8 or/and 9.)

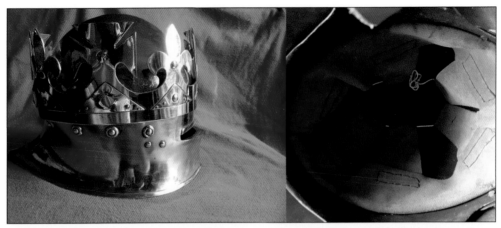

A Sallet helmet showing the padding inside, putting a space between your skull and the actual metal.

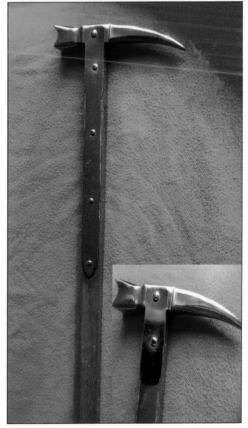

Left: A rondel dagger. *Right*: A war hammer. Both objects have a lethal point.

Either way, I cannot believe that Richard could have been in such a situation that he had no helmet on and was sitting down on the ground, while someone with only a roundel dagger stood above him and banged the dagger on the top of his head with enough force to put it through the top of his skull. In addition, if by some fluke someone could have done that, surely there would be some form of mark on the opposite side of the inside of the skull, as with wound 6?

I think that when wound 4 was inflicted, Richard still had his helmet on. He may have been struggling to breath and have been disoriented, and this may well be why someone on horseback was able to come up behind him and strike him cleanly on his helmet with a war hammer. I agree completely with Robert Woosnam-Savage that if Richard was not wearing a helmet, a war hammer would make a very different hole in a skull, but if someone was wearing a helmet the point of the hammer would be stopped by the helmet itself. As there is a space and padding between the metal and the top of the wearer's head, only the point would penetrate the skull. The point of the war hammer is wedge-shaped. The helmet would slow the speed and reduce the force of the impact but enough of the point could have gone through the metal and the padding to impact on the skull just enough to cause the injury seen on the skeleton. This surely would have been enough to cause Richard to collapse, and perhaps even fall into unconsciousness, allowing him to have his helmet pulled off (or cut off) before people attacked him from behind with a halberd and sword.

Whatever the truth – and I expect we will never know either how he really died or by whose hand – we do know that he fought to the end, and with his death the Plantagenet kings' line died too. Henry Tudor, Earl of Richmond, was now king. The Tudor line would run for another 120 years and change the face of England, and the world, for ever.

Chapter 11

Percy, Earl of Northumberland

Some people describe Henry Percy, Earl of Northumberland as a coward, while others call him an out-and-out traitor to Richard. I think both of these statements are unjust. Potential evidence of his allegiance to Richard was the fact that Percy was arrested not long after the battle, along with Ralph Neville, 3rd Earl of Westmorland and Thomas Howard, Earl of Surrey, then 2nd Duke of Norfolk (after his father had been killed in the battle). He was still nominally imprisoned for several months but eventually, having sworn allegiance to the new king, Henry VII released him on terms of good behaviour. Percy was allowed to retain his titles and lands as well as returning to his previous posts.

As shown in the previous chapters, the events surrounding the death of Richard III were probably played out in minutes rather than hours. Richard may have started his final charge with a slow measured walk but in less than 6 minutes he was unseating Sir John Cheney. No sooner had he started hand-to-hand fighting than Sir William Stanley (and potentially Rhys ap Thomas and mercenaries) joined Henry's ranks and pushed Richard some 600m back to the mire. This may have been no more than 10 minutes from when he started his charge.

If Stanley only moved his mounted contingent east in an arc, leaving his foot soldiers still on the rise facing Percy and in full view, as I suggest, it may well have been to shield his cavalry from not only from Richard's view, but also from Percy's. An added disadvantage may also have been that Percy did not even know that there was a mounted force with Stanley, at least not until they were actually joining Henry's contingent, to what may well have been his far right-hand side, and nearly 1½km away.

Thus, Percy would have had less than 5 minutes to gather his forces, which may well have numbered as many as 7,000, change their point of direction by possibly as much as 135 degrees and then to prepare them to move forward to protect his king. Not only that, but Percy would have quickly seen Richard and his men struggling in the mire and found himself facing a huge dilemma – how could he get to his king and how could he do so while avoiding the marsh and getting trapped himself?

Looking at the ridge and furrow map again (opposite), however, it is not clear which areas would have been sown areas and which areas would have been pasture. By 1485 the 'Black Death', or bubonic plague, had ravaged Europe with an estimated number of deaths somewhere between 75,000,000 and 200,000,000. In England between 1348 and 1353 it is estimated that 40–60 per cent of the population contracted the disease. In 1361–2 a second outbreak caused a further 20 per cent of the remaining population to die. This meant that land that was farmed before the outbreak was far greater than the land that was either able to be farmed or indeed needed to be farmed. The result of this meant that the early medieval ridge and furrow would have been allowed to turn into rough pasture, or if poor quality ground, simply back to scrub.

As suggested earlier, further auguring may well be able to identify more of the extent of the late medieval marsh, and possibly which areas of ground were still under cultivation during this specific period. Trying to turn troops within a crop of 3ft wheat would have been even slower than moving troops on scrub. The main purpose of creating such a map would be to aid future research into the battlefield within its medieval landscape. The relevance of the 'marsh or mire' within the context of the battle seems to be of such importance to the outcome. However, there is so little or no visual evidence today within the modern landscape due mainly to Victorian and subsequent drainage that a fuller examination would give researchers an unparalleled understanding of the landscape in 1485.

A map showing the ridge and furrow and alluvium deposits in the area of Fenn Lane created throughout the whole of the medieval period.

Based on information gained by AHARG when looking for the potential marsh originally, deposits of peat were found in intermittent locations across the landscape. When the samples were looked at by experts at both Birmingham Archaeo-Environmental and the Division of Archaeological, Geographical & Environmental Sciences, School of Life Sciences at the University of Bradford they were found to be of differing ages. For example, the small area of peat found where Peter Foss had placed the marsh in his 1985 book was scientifically dated to have dried out in or around the seventh century. Using the two data sets of the alluvium deposits and the medieval ridge and furrow we can identify where potential areas of peat might be found. (An area of medieval marsh must be in alluvium and, by default, should not be found under medieval ridge and furrow.) However, at this time, the two data sets are nowhere near as accurate as this project actually needs, so there is a requirement for some careful fieldwork to be undertaken.

To create the map, it is suggested that a grid, initially based on a 10 metre square, is used. A hand-held auger can then be used on the intersection of each square, and each subsequent plug analysed for signs of peat. (If peat is found, the depth from the modern ground surface should also be logged.) However, any marsh or mire at Bosworth is not the same as the proverbial marsh on Bodmin. The marsh here at Bosworth would have potentially covered a large area (or more likely a number of large areas), however it would not have been a complete area of open marsh. It is far more likely that the area would have been made up of both wet, even, open water areas and drier areas. If this is true, and I think the small evidence we already have confirms this, the 10-metre-square grid would need to be at least reduced to a 2.5-metre-square grid – and once proven medieval peat is found that grid may well need to be reduced further to as little as 1-metre or even 0.5-meter-square grids.

I believe that by the time Percy had even started to understand these issues, devise and then relay his plans to his troops, Richard was probably already dead. It was not that he was a coward, but simply that events happened too quickly for him to be of any practical assistance. Philippa Langley adds, 'for Northumberland's part at Bosworth, it's interesting to note that his will is dated 27 July 1485 so it seems he intended to take part in the battle. Of the seventeen knights named in his will, ten are known to have fought for Richard III and the remaining seven seem not to have taken part, or aren't named in any extant sources.' (taken from:https://www.revealingrichardiii.com/case-study.html (part 4, n. 50)).

Chapter 12

The Immediate Aftermath

Richard III, the last of the medieval kings, was dead. The battle was over. Or at least technically. As soon as one of the main two protagonists was confirmed dead what was the point of continuing to fight, risking your own life, the life of your colleagues and friends?

However as with most battles, there is always the opportunity for recompense and profit. The losing army would be routed. The losing soldiers would know this and would therefore try and make their way back to their camp, pick up what they could and then make good their escape. Once clear of the battlefield and given enough time the average person would probably be safe. (More high-ranking commanders might still be worth capture.) However, while still 'on the field' anyone was fair game.

During some of the most recent research in 2021 evidence has been uncovered that might pinpoint where at least some of the fighting during the rout took place. One of the objects found is what is thought to be part of a quillon, or more accurately a cross-guard. It is either a piece towards the end of a sword cross-guard, or more likely from a dagger cross-guard. It has been broken at both ends, has a triangular cross-section and is made of copper alloy (bronze). At the time of its discovery, there were no obvious signs of any gilding, silvering or enamelling, however it would need to be cleaned under laboratory conditions to know for certain. Along with all the finds from this particular project, this piece went to the University

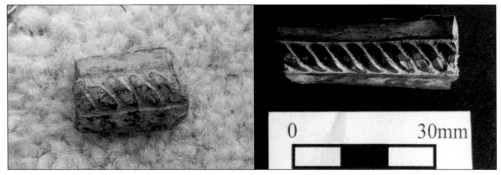

Left: Part of a potential dagger cross-guard made from bronze found at the site of the rout near Richard's camp site and the village of Sutton Cheney. *Right*: Part of a cross-guard – as identified by the Royal Armouries. This is from a high-status sword and is made from bronze and gilded. It was found at the site of the clash between Richard and Henry.

of Leicester Archaeological Services (ULAS). However, what was immediately obvious was that it was very similar to an object that we had found out on the western edge of the battle site back in February 2010 and identified by experts from the Royal Armouries, Leeds. Both are from high-status weapons.

A cross-guard's primary function is to protect the user's hand and fingers from an opponent's blade, especially when it is being parried, i.e. blade on blade. A cross-guard needs to be strong and not be prone to breaking. It is normally therefore made of steel. However, in both these cases the cross-guard fragments are made of copper alloy which is intrinsically brittle. Why would anyone choose to go into battle with a weapon that was potentially not safe? More importantly, who would go into battle with such a weapon? The answer must be a person or persons of wealth, but also, someone whose chosen weapons did not include a sword – or at least not this sword. This sword and dagger (if that is what it is from) must have been for show or possibly ceremonial purposes. Some of the other pieces found near the dagger cross-guard included two harness fitments also made of copper alloy. None of these finds categorically give us a 'stand-and-hold' style of rout, nor an out-and-out 'flee from the field', but I would suggest that it would always be safer to try and keep groups of men together. Stand and face the enemy while another group falls back.

Though Henry's coronation in Westminster Abbey would not be until 30 October 1485, he was still the new king as soon as Richard died. Tradition has it that Richard's crown or diadem was found in a thorn bush by Sir Reginald Bray,

Left: A mount with a face, similar to three found at Towton. *Right*: A heraldic stud with an unknown coat of arms.

who handed it to Sir William Stanley (according to Fabian). Vergil, who wrote much later and after Sir William's execution, puts the crown in Thomas Stanley's hands. Either way, we are then given some options as to what happens next. Some state that Henry went to either the nearest high ground or a nearby hill. According to the 'Ballad of Bosworth', it was to 'a mountayne hyghe'. Holinshed states Henry went to 'the top of a littell mountaine'. More recently some people put the actual crowning at or very near the current site of Crown Hill Farm.

What we do know for certain is that in the Act of Enclosure of 1605 the hill known as Crown Hill lay in the great field of Crown Hill Field. More importantly it had been given this name at some point between 1467/8 and 1605. Prior to 1468, the hill had been known as Garbrodys and the great field that encompassed the north-western part of the township, and borders the area of known roundshot, was named Garbrodfelde. I think we can rule out the farm from the possible options because if Henry and his loyal contingent had moved from where Richard potentially fell, and therefore lost his diadem, to the farm – which is a distance of over 1,200m – surely he would have gone another 400m to the Church of St Margaret (of Antioch)? He was after all king as an act of God. Today this church still bears signs of its early thirteenth-century origins. It underwent extensive enlargement between 1290 and

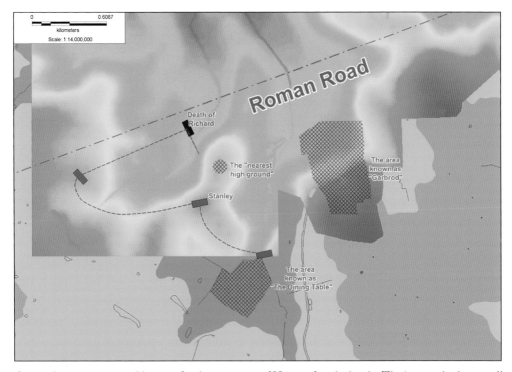

A map showing two possible areas for the crowning of Henry after the battle. The 'nearest high ground' to the marsh is close to the centre of the map, the larger highlighted area to the east is the area previously known as 'Garbrod'.

1340 when the south aisle and Lady Chapel and the tower and spire were added. The chancel was widened in the fourteenth century, and then was subsequently rebuilt in 1882 when it acquired the pitched roof.

If my positioning of Stanley 'between the two armies' is correct, it would be a logical hypothesis to suggest that Stanley went to the nearest high ground (simply, dry ground out of the mire) to crown Henry as King of England. This needs to be only a total of 500m from where Richard fell. Once he had been seen by his followers as the rightful king, then, and only then, would it have been a case of moving less than 1,000m to an area over the brow of the hill to his camp for refreshment out of sight of the dead and dying. This area is still to this day known by some locals as the 'Dining Table'. This area has never knowingly been comprehensively metal-detected, however, some years ago an independent detectorist found a gold coin of Edward IV that could well have been either 'camp litter' or deliberately buried before the battle by one of Stanley's men.

The crowning of Henry Tudor, from *After the Battle of Bosworth*, J.R.S.C., ed. J. Erskine Clarke (1899).

The battle was over and a new age, the Tudor Age, was beginning. The truth of what actually happened began to slide from memory and gradually became lost, even the battlefield itself disappeared for centuries until now. But it was there, just below the surface, waiting to be rediscovered. This, then, is my hypothesis of what happened during that iconic battle, based on the remains we have found and what we have recently learned. You might not be convinced by all you have read, but what we can all agree on with certainty is that there is more out there, waiting to be discovered. This book has been written to encourage all to question what has gone before, to enter a discussion with an open mind and set aside preconceived ideas. Ultimately, we are just simply seeking the truth as to what happened on this historic day – whatever that may be.

Chapter 13

An Alternative Interpretation

Henry Tudor, Earl of Richmond was in the vicinity of the battle area for some time before the 22nd, while King Richard III only arrived in Leicester at the earliest on the 19th, making his way to the area of the final battle on the eve of the event itself. Therefore, was Henry being pulled into a trap or was *he* actually encouraging Richard into something of his own planning?

Both commanders knew that Henry would have to stand and fight. Henry knew he would not be able to make his way down Watling Street towards London without having his rear constantly harassed by Richard. Richard knew that, if no one else did, and Oxford was far too competent a general to allow Henry to make such a fundamental error or to even try and attempt to flee back to Wales. Without a doubt, both men would have known at least on the Sunday evening that battle would commence on the Monday.

The question is, therefore, is there any evidence to prove either way who chose the ground? We suspect that Henry knew John Hardwick, who owned Lindley Hall, which was just south of the present Fenn Lane and east of the village of Fenny Drayton. It is also near to the green lane that runs from Sheepy. We also know that Henry had at least one meeting with Sir William Stanley prior to the 22nd. Did Henry (and Sir William) set a trap for Richard by positioning themselves deliberately in the landscape to entice Richard into a specific area of landscape?

Henry knew Richard would need a road to effectively move his troops around the landscape as he could not easily travel across areas of ground still covered in 3ft-high wheat. To get from Leicester to Watling Street (the current A5), there were only a handful of options that Richard and his troops could have taken. Therefore, a secondary, but equally as important, question is, could Henry steer Richard to a specific route so he would walk into Henry's pre-prepared trap?

If Henry's commanders were setting a trap, it was a bold and potentially fatal plan. Richard still had far more troops under his control. It would require nerves of steel not only to put a smaller group of troops out in the open in front of the king, but Henry would have to be seen to be there as well. This would be the carrot to encourage Richard to charge across the landscape and commit himself, while the stick, Stanley, sat out of sight on the flank, to appear 'in the nick of time' and save Henry. This might be a romantic, Hollywood interpretation, and I suspect if even remotely accurate, Henry's poets and historians would have made sure it was recorded as Henry's master stroke. There were far too many opportunities for it all to go horribly wrong.

Would Norfolk move out to attack Oxford? If he did not, the plan would probably fail. Would Richard charge Henry? If he did not, the plan would probably fail. If Stanley misjudged his appearance, the plan would probably fail. If Henry's mercenary support wavered, the plan would probably fail. If Richard charged, and hit Henry rather than his banner bearer, the plan would catastrophically fail! On the other hand, did Richard pick the site of the battle? If Richard knew that he was always wanting to undertake a massed mounted charge, Richard would know that he would need a gently sloping open landscape, with Henry sitting at the bottom of that slope. With his revolutionary new field cannon, Richard would know that he would need a gently sloping open landscape, with Henry sitting at the bottom of that slope. With the uncertainty of his support, Richard wanted an event that would be both quick and decisive, and most importantly – in his favour.

Was this area that best landscape? The landscape is actually a huge bowl with the current Fenn Lane Farm sitting quietly at the bottom. From this point everywhere is up. It is as much the 'Redmoor Bowl' as 'Redmoor Plane'.

If Henry had sat on the ridge rather than moving down the slope and the (current) Fenn Lane, Richard would have had to charge up the slope into Henry. It would have doubled the distance to Stanley's support and potentially would have caused Richard to not undertake his charge, so he was obliged to expose himself as the inexperienced Welsh pretender, who made a fateful mistake, came off the rim, and stopped in the bottom of the bowl facing his nemesis who also had a larger force. It was a major gamble. All his eggs were in one basket – or was that one bowl!

A 10m contour map showing the 'Redmoor Bowl'.

Chapter 14

Understanding the Roundshot

Until we found the first roundshot at Bosworth, I think it would be fair to say that no one expected any evidence of artillery. However, having discovered that initial scatter of balls by 2010, some people have seemingly based their whole interpretation of the Bosworth Campaign on that small (but by no means insignificant) scatter.

The University of Leeds's website goes as far to state that although handguns and hand cannon firing balls up to as much as 30mm had become commonplace in European armies by the late fifteenth century, the discovery of shot larger than that proves that Bosworth is the first recorded battle in England to use mobile artillery pieces. Time and research on earlier Wars of the Roses battle sites will prove if this is indeed the case. However, an article describing the Battle of Barnet written by David Ross for the website *Britain Express*, www.britainxxpress.com, states:

> … Warwick's men were already in position when Edward's army arrived on the night of April 13 [1471]. Edward disposed his troops in the dark, intending to repel an expected attack at dawn. In the dark he misjudged the distance between his men and the enemy, and drew up much closer to Warwick than he intended. It proved to be a fortunate error, for the Lancastrian artillery kept up a constant barrage during the night, but overshot the mark almost completely, so Edward's army was intact when the dawn came.

I hope, nonetheless, that in the previous pages I have based my hypothesis on more evidence than just those lead alloy spheres. That said, trying to understand

Five roundshot found in August 2016.

the implications of the lead shot is extremely important, not only in trying to work out their importance on the late medieval battlefield or even who used artillery at Bosworth, but in ultimately assessing who had what gun and where exactly in the landscape were they positioned. It is only on reassessing the finds data that one starts, potentially, to understand what might have been going on.

A map showing all confirmed battle finds as of January 2021 – confirmed roundshot in red and all others in green.

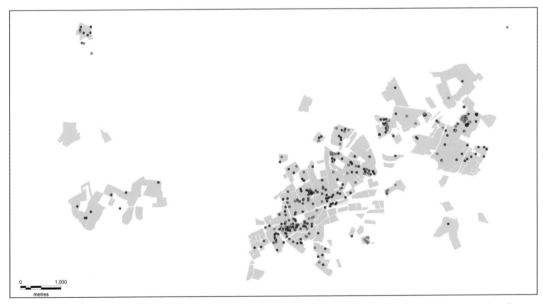

A map showing all potential battle finds as of January 2021 in blue – confirmed roundshot in red and confirmed finds in green.

The first map opposite shows all the objects found up to January 2021, during the research project, that are thought definitely to have been lost at the time of the battle. There seems to be a cluster around Fenn Lane and Fenn Lane Farm. However, other potential scatters can be made out to the south and east of the village of Sutton Cheney. There is a less obvious grouping between Apple Orchard Farm and Mill Cottage, Shenton.

The map below opposite adds to those finds with up to 206 extra objects thought to be potentially from the battle. Theses finds include things such as mounts, buckles and certain coinage. One of the other interesting finds is a lead inkwell, found in the area of Henry's line.

The map overleaf shows the confirmed fired roundshot positioned within those scatters. It suggests at least one (though I have already suggested that there are at least two) areas of fighting around the Fenn Lane Farm area. As of 2020, there is a total of forty-three confirmed shot one of which is to the north west (an unfired

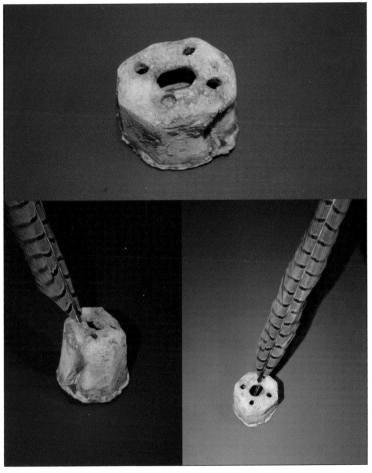

A lead inkwell – with a modern pheasant feather quill.

A map showing all confirmed battle finds including lead balls 20mm or larger. The arrow highlights one new sphere which may or may not be medieval.

shot found in Henry's campsite). These vary in size from 20mm diameter and 53g up to 97mm diameter and 3,577g. However, a lot more lead spheres have been found during the survey. In fact, over 270. These have been previously classified as simply 'balls', and have been given the period date of 'post medieval'. The question is are those actually 'post-medieval' finds, or should some at least be re-classified as being from the battle?

The map above shows the same roundshot with the addition of any other balls of 20mm diameter or more. In this case there is only one additional ball, highlighted with an arrow. In this case there is only one additional ball, highlighted with an arrow. Among the battle finds in the fields due east of the village of Sutton Cheney, the proposed site for Richard's overnight camp, is a ball with major impact measuring 20.34mm but weighing only 25.03g was found. Could this be another medieval roundshot? Left, unfired, lying in the grass of the campsite after the men had moved off on that Monday morning? The major impact in this case not caused by firing but by a more modern tractor and plough? Or could it be a Tudor roundshot, fired into the camp of their enemy during the rout after the battle? The third option is it is not from the medieval period at all and is a more modern, smaller projectile that has been badly malformed.

The map opposite now has a further fifteen balls added in black including two between 19mm and 19.99mm, and five between 18.50mm and 18.99mm diameter.

A map showing all confirmed battle finds including lead balls 18mm or larger. Those 18.00 to 19.99mm are in black.

This puts another two balls in the area of the suspected Oxford/Norfolk clash. Two on the western edge of the suspected Henry/Richard clash and three more in Richard's campsite." However, on the flip side to this argument there are also two balls just to the east of the village of Sutton Cheney. Are these also balls from the battle or are they actually from a later period and fired by local poachers?

The ultimate 'fire storm'.

A map showing all confirmed battle finds including lead balls 16mm or larger.

A map showing all confirmed battle finds including lead balls 14mm or larger.

The table opposite details the various gauge sizes with weights for solid lead spheres. The bores marked * are found in punt guns and rare weapons only. The .410 bore and 23mm calibre are exceptions; they are actual bore sizes, not gauges. If the .410 and 23mm were measured traditionally, they would be 67.62 gauge and 6.278 gauge, respectively.

Gauge	Diameter		Weight of Unalloyed (Pure) Lead Ball		
(bore)	(mm)	(in)	grams	ounces	grains
AA*	101.60	4.000	6225.52	219.600	96,080
A½*	76.20	3.000	2626.39	92.640	40,530
0.25*	67.34	2.651	1814.36	64.000	28,000
0.5*	53.45	2.103	907.18	32.000	14,000
A*	50.80	2.000	778.19	27.450	12,010
0.75*	46.70	1.838	604.80	21.336	9,328
1*	42.42	1.669	453.59	16.000	7,000
B½*	38.10	1.500	328.30	11.580	5,066
1.5*	37.05	1.459	302.39	10.667	4,667
2*	33.67	1.326	226.80	8.000	3,500
3*	29.41	1.158	151.20	5.333	2,333
4*	26.72	1.052	113.40	4.000	1,750
B*	25.40	1.000	97.27	3.430	1,501
5*	24.80	0.976	90.72	3.200	1,400
6*	23.35	0.919	75.60	2.667	1,166
6.278	23.00	0.906	72.26	2.549	1,114
7*	22.18	0.873	64.80	2.286	1,000
8	21.21	0.835	56.70	2.000	875
9*	20.39	0.803	50.40	1.778	778
10	19.69	0.775	45.36	1.600	700
11*	19.07	0.751	41.24	1.454	636
12	18.53	0.729	37.80	1.333	583
13*	18.04	0.710	34.89	1.231	538
14	17.60	0.693	32.40	1.143	500
15*	17.21	0.677	30.24	1.067	467
16	16.83	0.663	28.35	1.000	438
17*	16.50	0.650	26.68	0.941	412
18*	16.19	0.637	25.20	0.889	389
20	15.63	0.615	22.68	0.800	350
22*	15.13	0.596	20.62	0.728	319
24	14.70	0.579	18.90	0.667	292
26*	14.31	0.564	17.44	0.615	269
28	13.97	0.550	16.20	0.571	250
32	13.36	0.526	14.17	0.500	219
36	12.85	0.506	12.59	0.444	194
40	12.40	0.488	11.34	0.400	175
67.62	10.41	0.410	6.71	0.237	104

Note: Using the table on the previous page to estimate bullet masses for historical large-bore rifles is limited, as it assumes the use of round ball rather than conical bullets. For example, a typical 4-bore rifle from *c.* 1880 used a 2,000-grain (4.57oz) bullet, or sometimes slightly heavier, rather than a 4oz round lead ball. (Round balls give progressively much worse external ballistic performance than conical bullets at ranges greater than about 75yd.) In contrast, a 4-bore express rifle often used a 1,500-grain (3.43oz) bullet wrapped in paper to keep lead build-up to a minimum in the barrel. In either case, assuming a 4oz mass for a 4-bore rifle bullet from this table would be inaccurate, although indicative.

Handgonne calibre can go up to 32mm (there is an example in the Danish War Museum) but many late fifteenth-century examples from the Continent are in the 20 to 25mm range. There is an early serpentine matchlock from the early 1500s in Croatia which is 35mm (Croatian History Museum, Zagreb). Anything more than 40mm is definitely from a carriage field piece. Anything less than 20mm is definitely a handgonne or an early harquebus. Anything between 20 and 30mm is more than likely a handgonne, and anything between 30 and 40mm could be a large handgonne or a small carriage field piece.

James Green, a highly experienced and well-regarded re-enactor master gunner, has suggested that a lot would depend on the weight of the barrel. He has studied many contemporary illustrations and analysed how the guns were supported while being fired. Hook guns are reasonably obvious, along with pole guns, and have the base of their stock braced against the ground. But Green also suggests that even a fit man would have enormous problems holding a weapon with a bore of 20mm to his shoulder, let alone one of 25mm, without the aid of some extra support, and profess to be aiming it at anything, let alone a specific group of enemy, such as a small block of mobile billmen. While some of the smaller size shot could have been fired from robinets or falconets as 'bag shot' like a giant shotgun, it is most likely, unless you find a very high concentration of smaller balls in a given area not a broad-fronted line, that they were shot from hand-held guns up to 20mm diameter. It is less clear with 20mm to 38mm spheres, but most probably these would be fired from a small, wheeled gun supported by some frame-like tripod such as an A frame, forked stick or Pavese shield. Anything from 38mm upwards would be from a wheeled carriage gun. The table opposite lists types of cannon in use in England during the sixteenth and seventeenth centuries.

Names	Bore of Cannon in	Weight of Cannon lb	Weight of Shot lb	Weight of Powder lb
Cannon-royal	8.50	8,000	66.00	50.00
Cannon	8.00	6,000	60.00	47.00
Cannon serpentine	7.00	5,500	53.50	25.00
Bastard-cannon	7.00	4,500	41.00	20.00
Demi-cannon	6.75	4,000	33.50	18.00
Cannon-petro	6.00	4,000	24.50	14.00
Culverin	5.50	4,500	17.50	12.00
Basilisk	5.00	4,000	15.00	10.00
Demi-culverin	4.00	3,400	9.50	8.00
Bastard-culverin	4.00	3,000	5.00	5.25
Sacar	3.50	1,400	5.50	5.00
Minion	3.50	1,000	4.00	4.00
Falcon	2.50	660	2.00	3.50
Falconet	2.00	500	1.50	3.00
Serpentine	1.50	400	0.75	1.75
Rabinet	1.00	300	0.50	0.50

As I stated at the beginning of the is chapter, 'Until we found the first roundshot at Bosworth, I think it would be fair to say that no one expected any evidence of artillery …'. Now, (some) people are basing their whole interpretations on (in many cases) nothing more than thirty-four objects. But what technically is a roundshot?

A roundshot (sometimes called 'solid-shot' or simply 'ball') is simply nothing more than a solid spherical object, which does not have any explosive charge, that is launched from a gun. Its diameter is only slightly less than the bore of the barrel from which it is shot. Originally a roundshot was made from dressed stone, referred to as gunstone (Middle English gunneston, from gonne, gunne, gun + stoon, ston, stone). We know that there was also lead shot (solid and with stone, flint or iron inside). The cast-iron cannonball was introduced by a French artillery engineer, Samuel J. Besh, sometime after 1450. Initially it was used against enemy ships or fortifications as the most accurate projectile that could be fired by a smoothbore cannon. England could initially only import iron shot, until blast furnaces were built here, and casters learnt the techniques in the mid-sixteenth century. What is the possibility that along with the lead spheres there were either stone or iron shot being fired across the field at Bosworth?

Iron shot was very much in its infancy and as it is a large chunk of iron, if there had been any fired at Bosworth we would hopefully have found at least one with a metal detector. Stone shot obviously cannot be found using a metal detector. Over

A modern reproduction wheeled carriage gun.

the years one or two iron spheres have been presented to the battlefield heritage centre. All of these have been identified, however, by 'experts' as industrial balls. (A lot of crusher mills used round iron ball to crush rock, coal etc. They were also used as ball bearings.) The only way to find a 500-year-old stone shot in the field is to physically see it on the ground – this is of course assuming that it was still a sphere and not damaged beyond recognition due to 500-plus years of weathering or plough damage – let alone impact damage after the initial firing.

Stone shot has been carved from a hard form of limestone known as Kentish Ragstone, one of the few hard stones found in southern England. However, they have also been cut from limestone from Dundry near Bristol, and some of a dense greeny-grey sandstone which could be from Somerset or South Wales. I would suggest that any good-quality carving stone would be used, especially during time of conflict or when reserves were low.

No stone shot has been found on Bosworth – or at least not knowingly! However, in September 2020, the Bosworth team of detectorists was undertaking some initial survey work looking for evidence of the Battle of Losecoat Field, 1470. The story of this battle is that King Edward IV's scouts informed him that the rebel army was about 5 miles from Stamford, arrayed for battle beside the Great North Road to the north of Tickencote Warren, near Empringham in Rutland. Edward positioned his men in a battle line to the north of Welles's army, and then, in the space separating the two forces, had Lord Welles executed in sight of both armies. This action set the rebels advancing with cries of 'á Warwick' and 'á Clarence'. A single barrage of cannonballs was fired and then Edward had his men charge towards the enemy. Before the leaders of this attack could even come to blows with the rebel front line, the battle was over. The rebels broke and fled rather than face the king's highly trained men. Like so many of the other Wars of the Roses's battles, Losecoat is a battle that is difficult to place with any certainty within the landscape. On the first day of our team's initial metal-detecting survey among a couple of interesting finds the stone sphere seen below was found. The question is, is it a stone roundshot?

A potential stone shot? This was found by the author on Losecoat Field in September 2020.

One other type of object that has been found (in small numbers) over the area of Bosworth is flint spheres. The big question is, though, would these natural objects have been used as an offensive weapon? Flint is fossilised sponge and flint spheres are known as 'Type B' flint; 'B' is for ball. According to Russell Yeomans, and after many years research, these particular flints are a fairly common find at Sidestrand beach in Norfolk and West Runton, North Norfolk. They range in size between 105mm down to 38mm diameter. They will often show a 'nostril' where the sponge is beginning to emerge frequently showing more than one exit hole for the tail(s).

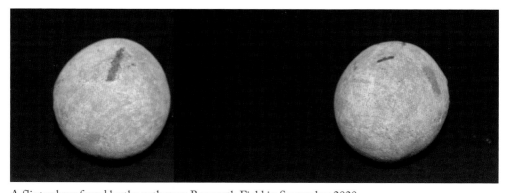

A flint sphere found by the author on Bosworth Field in September 2020.

The big question is would a gunner put a piece of flint down a gun barrel. The answer seems to be very much split. Some say, no way would anyone put something down a barrel that was not perfectly spherical as it would damage the inside of your barrel. If you fired a piece of flint it would more than likely shatter; either in the barrel, or as it leaves it. In response others suggest, as long as you wad the 'ball' with grass or cloth, it does not need to be a completely perfect sphere. If the flint shatters as it leaves the barrel, you have instant grapeshot – you hit more people in the enemy ranks.

A single stone shot would have taken many hours for a skilled craftsman to make. Some of the stone would shatter while carving due to faults within the stone, making it useless. As the importance of gunpowder weapons increased on the battlefields of the War of the Roses, technology had to play catchup. More and more research is being undertaken on many of the battles of this period. However, only one lead roundshot has been found from the Battle of Northampton, 1460. One potential stone shot has been found from Losecoat, 1470. One lead roundshot has been found from Towton, 1461 (from the thousands of other battle finds from this site). Three lead shot have reportedly been found from Barnet, 1471, and three from Flodden, 1513. Between Barnet, 1471, and Flodden, 1513, we have Bosworth, 1485, and we now have over forty lead shot. Obviously, some of this is due to the intensive survey work undertaken at Bosworth in comparison with that at the Northampton battlefield, for example. However, in contrast there has been as much work at Towton as at Bosworth. I would suggest that the crossover from stone shot to lead to iron was slow but steady. Even as late as the mid-sixteenth century stone, lead and iron was clearly still in use, as evidenced by the warship *Mary Rose*, which was lost in 1545 and salvaged in 1982 with examples of stone, lead and iron shot onboard.

Again, as with many things with battlefield research, there is much work still to do to more fully understand the details.

Chapter 15

Eliminating the Options

A t the very beginning of this book I said that I was hoping that what people might do in reading this book would be to question what has gone before, to enter into a discussion with an open mind and to set aside preconceived ideas. I went on to quote Sir Arthur Conan Doyle, 'When you have eliminated the impossible, whatever remains, however improbable, must be the truth.' I would, however, still suggest a more practical saying would be, 'If everything else is found to be unlikely, what is left must be the most likely.' I might also add, 'Half the battle in battlefield research, is to find where there was *no* battle.' However, I would also temper both those comments by adding the statement, 'To truly understand what has gone before, one must first fully understand how the evidence has been sought.' I have tried to look at some of the main aspects around the battle with no preconceived ideas, to look at the evidence and draw conclusions for what may have happened.

'History is fact – only the interpretation keeps changing.'

It may now be possible to look at other historians and authors and, politely, suggest why I believe the increased information resource pool brings into question the validity of some of their points. At no time am I ever implying people have deliberately proposed that an event did or did not take place in a certain area incorrectly. It is rather that as additional information comes to light, the more the interpretation can be fine-tuned.

As an example, most historians had always agreed with each other that Richard camped on Ambion Hill. Indeed, some even suggested that Richard charged from the hill down to his death near the current Shenton Station. Henry was frequently stated to have camped at Whitemoors, between the village of Shenton and Fenn Lane. However, we all know now this cannot be true – for we have found archaeological evidence which indisputably rejects Whitemoors as Henry's campsite and hopefully I have offered enough evidence to now seriously question the location of Richard's camp.

A more difficult and far more recent theory is that put forward by Mike Ingram in his excellent book *Richard III and the Battle of Bosworth*. He states that he has used the archaeological data to put together his interpretation of the layout of the

The map on the left shows the current true battle find spots. The map on the right is Ingram's suggested lines for Richard (purple) and Henry (green).

various armies within the landscape. He very eloquently proposes that the armies drew up opposite each other with the road running between them from left to right:

> Crucial to the understanding of the battle and how it unfolded was the discovery of a line of battle debris, running almost parallel with, and south of the old Roman road. The line was around 1,240 yards (1,132 metres) long, starting in the east with the now famous gilt boar badge close to the site of the now drained marsh known as Fen Hole. The line included coins, buckles, strap fittings, buttons and studs, a fragment of a gilded copper alloy cross-guard and a copper alloy chape from a sword scabbard, with the largest amount being found at the western end of the line. This must, therefore, be the line where the two battle-lines clashed in the hand-to-hand combat and suggests that the heaviest fighting occurred at the western edge.

The map on the left above shows the true battle find spots for the area around what is assumed to be the main location of the fighting. The map on the right above highlights what Mike Ingram suggests are possibly the lines of Richard's troops in purple and Henry's troops in green. However, if one increases the visual area of the map it can be clearly seen that though the two areas of concentrations still exist, they are not *as obvious*. There seems to be a bit of a concentration to the north of Ingram's Ricardian line, and a concentration off towards the north-east corner of the map, adjacent to Sutton Cheney. This can be seen in the map opposite. However, I feel it is a bold statement to make when these finds are not put into their full context.

In 2010 English Heritage re-classified the Battlefield Registration Area from the Battle of Bosworth. This area was 'created' on the back of the extensive survey work that I had been personally involved with. However, in 2019 I was detecting in a field outside the current registration area and found a previously undiscovered medieval roundshot. Therefore, when one looks at a nice white map with some fancy dots on it does that mean that there are no other finds in any of those fields where there are no dots – or does it simply mean that those areas have actually never been looked in?

A map showing the true battle finds as of 2021 in the wider landscape, highlighting the full spread and potentially less obvious concentrations.

Even if there has been work undertaken in a particular area has everything been found? We discovered the first roundshot in October 2008. The same experienced team of metal-detectorists went back into that field on at least two more occasions searching at 2.5m transects over the next twenty-four months – nothing (literally) was found. Seven years later just before some wildfowl scrapes were dug we went back into those fields again and we found seven previously undiscovered roundshot, including one measuring 97mm in diameter. Metal-detecting, even on a 2.5m transect is not an exact science. There are a huge number of variables – soil condition, moisture content, when was it last ploughed, the depth of ploughing let alone the detector head has got to go over the object before it can be detected.

If we go back to the map, we can look at what areas have been detected and which ones have not. Looking at the map on the next page we can see the areas that have been detected by the research team between 1995 and 2020. The clear pattern of two bands now seems to be considerbly less clear. One further consideration that should not be forgotten is that some of the ground has only been detected using 10m transects rather than the more intensive 2.5m that we now consistently use.

When the team originlly started looking for evidence of the battle we were like most others metal-detectorists – we simply wandered around an area until we either gave up or ran out of time. However, we quickley realised that this was not going to work so changed to walking a fixed grid pattern of one line every 20m. In 2005 this detected 10m grids then 5m and ultimatley 2.5m transects. In some areas we have even come down to 1.25m transects. If you ignore the random method, even

A map showing the true battle finds as of January 2021, with all detected areas highlighted in grey shown in the wider context.

though some battle finds were located using this method, the difference between 2.5m and 10m transects is 4 to 1. In other words, you could expect to discover four times as many battle finds walking 2.5m transects as opposed to walking 10m transects.

A map showing the true battle finds as of January 2021, with only 2.5m transect detected areas highlighted in grey shown in the wider context.

The map below shows all of the battle finds again, however this time I have only highlighted the areas that have been walked at 2.5m transects (and sometimes more than once). There has been a total of almost exactly 500 acres (or 202 hectares) covered on the western side of the map. Within this there are a total of 67 finds, which works out at 7.46 confirmed battle finds per acre (or 2.65 per hectare).

To add an extra complication into the mix, one needs to question the definition of a battle find. In the years before the National Lottery Heritage Fund project of 2005–10 a number of items were found including some heraldic horse pendants. These were identified as belonging to a general family, but the 'experts' that we approached said that heraldic horse pendants had gone out of fashion by 1400. Therfore, it must just be coincedental that a non-local family was walking through the middle of nowhere with all their best family metal work on their horses and then coincidently a hundred years later the head of the same family just happens to be fighting over the same fields – but without the now unfashionable accoutrements.

Over 7,500 individual pieces of metal work have been located, mapped and bagged by the small group of dedicated metal-detectorists. Between 2005 and 2010 we walked the equivilant distance from Bosworth to Gibraltar and were on the way back! Each of those 7,500 finds has been looked at – and most have had some form of identification. However, it is not easy to confirm if an object was present at the battle or not. They can sometimes be difficult to date.

Today we like to put everything into nice neat little boxes, clearly defind. 'The medieval period finished with the death of Richard III on the afternoon of 22 August

A map showing the true battle finds as of January 2021, with only 2.5m transect detected areas highlighted in the main battle area.

1485 (at 10 minutes past 2) and the Tudor period followed on immediately.' However fashion does not change that quickly, or at least it did not then. The local village potter would carry on making the same style of pot, from the same source of clay that his father had taught him. He would carry on training his son to make those same pots as well, at least until some 'foreigner' wandered through the village with all his bits and bobs, and one of the nosey wives got a glimpse of a different style of pot and demanded that the local potter needed to make one like that as well.

Consequently, when the finds were identified, they were given one of three classifications – True Battle Finds, Possible Battle Finds and Non-Battle Finds. We know that seventy-six True Battle Finds were identified within the immediate area, however you can nearly double that with a further sixty finds that have been identified as Possible Battle Finds. Once all of these are plotted on the map it becomes nearly impossible to see any clear lines for Richard's and/or Henry's positions running parallel to Fenn Lane. This is only compounded when the mapped area is increased outwards to include the ground as far east as Shenton and Sutton Cheney. What the mapping tells us most is that there are not any real clearly defined areas of frontage or even clearly defined concentrations of battle debris, but that more systematic survey work needs to be carried out to find actually where there was no battle. What is far from clear is if the true finds continue out of the 'main area of battle' – or are there some distinct, stand-alone areas where potentially different things went on?

The other issue is to try and confirm if any of the Possible Battle Finds are in fact True Battle Finds. The database of examples of dateable finds from this period and more importantly from battles of this period was limited ten to fifteen years ago – and it is still far from vast. However, it now means finds from Bosworth can be compared with those of finds from Towton, Barnet, Flodden and, of course, those held in both the Royal Armouries in England as well as collections abroad.

Chapter 16

A Self-guided Trail Around the
Key Areas of the Battle of Bosworth, 1485

B osworth could be fairly described as a small battle, and it certainly only lasted for a relatively short time. Within days of the battle there was probably little sign that two kings had been there. However, for a number of generations the locals would have always known what had happened across those rolling fields at the end of the medieval period. As the years and centuries passed, memories faded and eventually people forgot where armies had come, fought and in many cases died.

In 2008, after a number of years of intensive search, the site of the battle was rediscovered by painstaking research. My interpretation of the battle is based on over twenty years of making archaeological finds and a personal knowledge of the landscape. In the description of the battlefield that follows, numbers in bold refer to points of interest on the modern map on the following page and in the story of the battle.

This trail has been designed for individuals, or small groups of people, to walk around the Battle of Bosworth, 1485. However, in the twenty-first century there are a number of potential threats that our medieval contemporaries would not have encountered. The most dangerous of these is the modern car. Where possible the route will follow old, traditional footpaths, but inevitably there is a certain amount of walking on roads, some of which modern cars travel along at speed. Therefore, please note:

- Negotiate all roads with great care.
- Where possible, always walk in single file, facing oncoming traffic.

When walking on dedicated footpaths please follow the Countryside Code:

- Keep to the footpath.
- It is recommended that dogs are not taken on the trail, as some of the stiles encountered are not pet friendly. However, if you do take pets, please keep them on a lead, especially if there is livestock in the field.

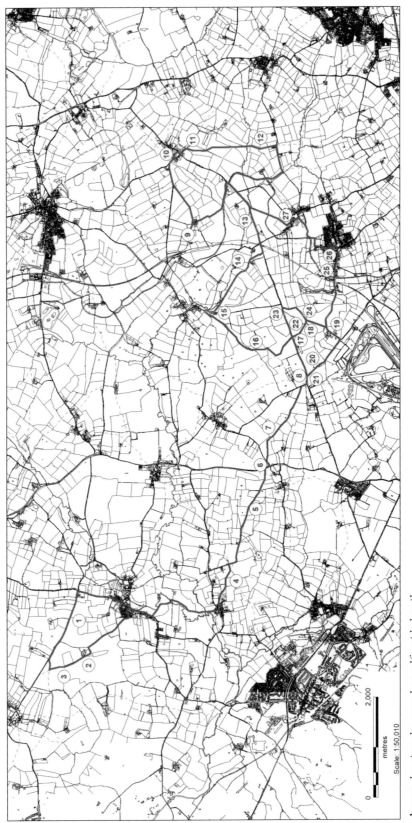

A map showing the complete self-guided trail.

This tour can be started at any point and undertaken in bite-size chunks. Or it can be completed in one circuit. However, due to the area covered, it is recommended that some form of transport will be required. The trail comprises the following sections:

- The Full Trail
- Henry's Camp
- Henry's Route to Battle
- Richard's Camp
- The Opening Salvoes
- The Death of Norfolk
- Richard's Charge
- Stanley's Opportunity
- Percy, Earl of Northumberland
- The Crowning of Henry Tudor
- Crown Hill
- Stoke Golding Church
- Dadlington Church
- Return to the Battlefield Heritage Centre

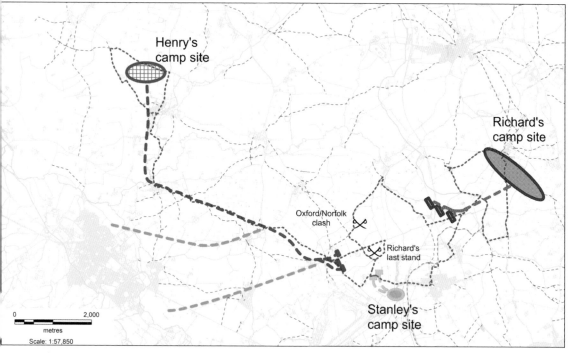

A map showing the complete battle layout.

Henry's Camp

There is no real way of knowing exactly where Henry was camped. Further work is needed, however, I would suggest that it was in or near the villages of Sheepy Magna and Sheepy Parva. There is also no certainty regarding the route he would have taken to reach the ultimate battle site. Unlike Richard, Henry's route to the site was a reasonably long one.

The route chosen to walk from Henry's probable campsite to the final battle site has been selected as the most direct one while still trying to keep to safer public footpaths and bridleways, rather than the more hazardous roads. Unfortunately, this part of the trail is reasonably lengthy and there is only a limited amount to see that could be deemed relevant to the battle. However, it is a route that gives the walker a good idea of what it might have been like for the common man preparing to fight for the pretender, Henry Tudor.

Starting point: Sheepy Magna village (layby off the B4116, Sheepy Magna)
Distance: 5.1km

Leave the village of Sheepy Magna and head off in a northerly direction along Twycross Road. Once you have left the village turn left at the 'Cross Hands' crossroads and follow Orton Lane. After approximately 500m pause at the field gate on your left and look back over the field. **Position 1. Henry's Campsite**.

Continue along Orton Lane for another 1,000m until you reach the bridleway on your left. Follow the bridleway out into the field for approximately 200m before turning left again and following the route of the public footpath towards the edge of the field and the right-hand corner of the wood situated in front of you. **Position 2. The Abbot's Summer Residence**.

Continue to follow the footpath past the wood and on towards the farm buildings. Pause at the brick barn. **Position 3. The Great Barn**.

Restart by keeping on the footpath towards the village. The path will take you along the edge of the fields before following the fringe of the village itself. Follow the waymarker route through the estate and make your way back to the centre of the village.

Position 1. Henry's Campsite
Look over the field gate and imagine to your front and stretching out to your right a sea of tents, horses, soldiers and smoky campfires. In these fields we have evidence of camp litter. Lost buckles and heraldic mounts have been found – as well as an unfired 40mm solid lead roundshot.

The modern trail around Henry's camp.

Position 2. The Abbot's Summer Residence

As you walk along the modern footpath towards the wood, look right to the stream and adjacent hedge. Beyond this 500-odd years ago you may well have seen the medieval hamlet of Weston. It is now the location of Moor Barns Farm. This is thought to have been the summer 'retreat' of the Abbot of Merevale Abbey. It was not unusual for the wealthier members of society to leave the more densely populated villages – or the abbey precincts – in a bid to avoid the stench and potential disease prevalent there.

If you look out along the footpath as you continue towards the modern wood in front of you, just below the horizon you should be able to pick out a large, pale spherical water tower on legs. This is situated on the outskirts of the town of Atherstone. Beyond the tower near the dip on the horizon is approximately the position of the Merevale Abbey.

Position 3. The Great Barn

The Great Barn at New House Grange is a large, medieval aisled barn and is said 'to have been the storehouse for the Leicestershire portion of the produce belonging to Merevale Abbey' (William White's *History, Gazetteer and Directory of the Counties of*

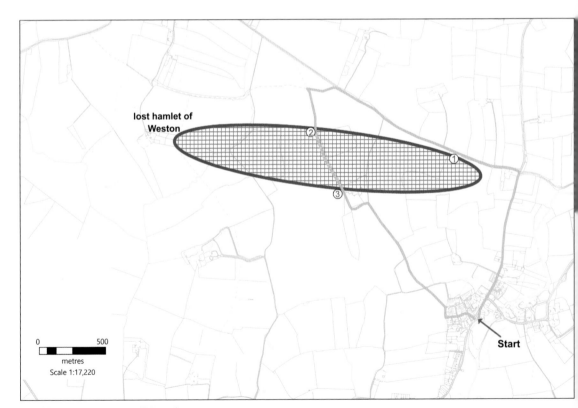

The interpretation of Henry's camp.

Leicester and Rutland (1863)). The definition of a grange is a barn belonging to 'the church' and filled with grain from 'church land' as opposed to a tithe barn, which is a barn filled with crops given to the church in lieu of tax. The barn you see today is timber-framed with eighteenth- and nineteenth-century brick infilling. However, it is thought to have been built originally in 1506 just after Henry VII visited (for the second time) to pay his recompense to the abbey for the damage to their crops.

The barn measures 44m long by 11.5m wide (144ft x 38ft). It is made up of six bays approximately 6.5m square (21ft square). The central truss divides the barn into two segments. The easternmost bay has a loft at the first-floor level that may have been the reeve's office. There are only about two-dozen such barns still in existence in the country – but this is one of the larger examples.

Henry's Route to Battle

Starting point: Sheepy Magna village (layby off the B4116, Sheepy Magna)
Distance: 7.3km

Leave the layby in the village of Sheepy Magna and this time head off in a southerly direction along the main road. After about 500m, take the waymarker footpath on the left (opposite residence number 94). Cross the field to the River Sence. Follow the riverbank for about 60m before turning right and walking along the path towards the corner of the field. Continue to the river again, and cross using the bridge and, following the footpath, turn right again.

Continue walking parallel with the river for about 350m, before the river meanders off to your right. Continue along the edge of the field, still in a southerly direction, until you get to another foot bridge – this time crossing the River Tweed. Follow the waymarker route into the village of Ratcliffe Culey. Cross the main road and walk up Omes Lane. After 50m continue onto the public footpath and into the field. Following the waymarker signs, cross the next five fields until you come out on the tarmacked road called Ratcliffe House Lane. **Position 4. View Towards Stoke Golding.**

Turn right and walk along the lane. Follow the lane as it turns left (away from the solar farm) crossing two cattle grids. Pass the buildings on your left and go through the field gate back into the fields. **Position 5. Henry's Route to the Battle.**

Pass the wood with it immediately on your right and continue following the green lane until you come out onto the main road. **Position 6. Witherly (Atterton) and Their Recompense.** This is the A444, Atherstone Road; please cross with extreme caution.

Walk up Upton Lane for 100m and re-join the green lane on the right. **Position 7. View Towards Market Bosworth.** Follow the lane to the end where it joins Stoke

The modern trail for Henry's route to battle.

Road. Turn right and follow it to the junction with Fenn Lane. Carefully cross the road and turn left and take the next junction on the right. **Position 8. Henry's Position Prior to Battle.**

Position 4. View Towards Stoke Golding
As you make your way over the fields you can look out across them and see the church spire of Stoke Golding on the horizon. The Church of St Margaret of Antioch dates to the early thirteenth century and would have stood out as a marker for Henry and his troops as they made their way towards the battle.

Position 5. Henry's Route to the Battle
As you walk along the green lane you are following in the footsteps of Henry and his men.

Position 6. Witherley (Atterton) and Their Recompense
'Compensation Warrants' were issued to Merevale Abbey by the victorious king in November and December 1485, just three months after the battle. Part of the First Warrant reads: '... and to deliver the same [compensation] to certain townships

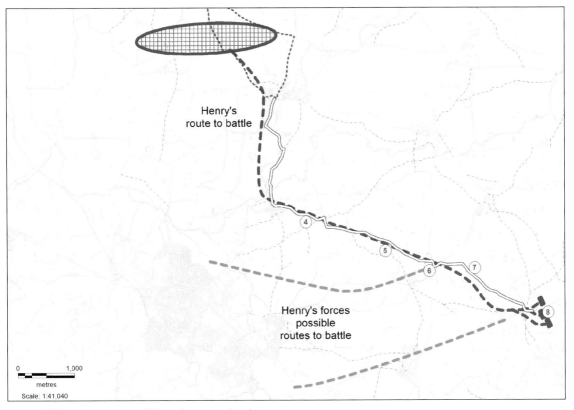

The interpretation of Henry's route to battle.

which sustained losses to their corns and grains by us and our company at our late victorious field for our due recompense on our behalf'.

The warrant goes on to mention Atherstone, Fenny Drayton, Witherley and Mancetter by name. The abbey was paid 100 marks in cash, with an additional 10 marks a short while later.

Here you are near the hamlet of Atterton. It is exceedingly small – with a population of approximately forty people. It is, however, part of the parish of Witherley, and as such some of Henry's men may well have joined the growing forces of the future king here before moving on to battle.

Position 7. View Towards Market Bosworth
Keep looking out slightly to the left of straight on and you will see the spire of St Peter's Church, Market Bosworth, again a church that Henry would have been able to see.

Position 8. Henry's Position Prior to Battle
This is the position that Henry reached immediately prior to the start of the battle. His enemy, Richard, was initially 5km away on the ridge at Sutton Cheney at his campsite, however, immediately before the battle they were less than 3km apart.

Richard's Camp

Starting point: Bosworth Battlefield Heritage Centre, Sutton Cheney
Distance: 6km

Starting from the centre's car park, move off in a north, north-west direction to the Battlefield Sundial and to where the battle standards of Richard and Henry are regularly flown. **Position 9. The Traditional Site.**

From here one can look north and see the spire of St Peter's Church, Market Bosworth. Panning left, if the sky is clear, near the horizon one can see the water tower at Atherstone. (It looks like a golf ball on sticks.) Behind this, and high on the skyline, is the (historical) site of Merevale Abbey. Looking through the picture-frame interpretation board, and in the near distance, Fenn Lane Farm can be seen.

The Sundial commemorates all those who died at the battle. From the Sundial turn 180 degrees and walk back through the car park and take the bridleway up along the ridge towards the village of Sutton Cheney. Continue along Ambion Lane. You will pass the Church of St James where a short detour will enable you to see a plaque donated by members of the Richard III Society in remembrance of Richard. **Position 10. Richard's Mass.**

Leave the church by the main path, cross the road and turn right passing the yard of Manor Farm. After 65m, turn left and walk down Twenty Acre Lane. At the

The modern trail for Richard's camp.

metal barrier turn right and take the footpath due south, and out across the fields for 1.8km. You will cross a grass trackway between the first and second field. Pause and look down the track towards the villages of Dadlington and Stoke Golding. **Position 11. Richard's Camp.**

Carry on along the footpath, crossing a stream and a number of stiles before leaving the fields next to New House Farm. Be careful as some of these stiles are not in perfect condition. **Position 12. The Alternative Ambion Hill.** As you exit the farm, turn right and walk down the road towards the village of Dadlington. Before crossing the stream take the footpath to the right across the next few fields. When you get to the farm road, turn left and walk up onto the bridge, before turning left again and dropping back down on to the canal, turning left for a third time and following the towpath all the way to Sutton Cheney Wharf.

Pass under the road bridge and then immediately take the steps on your left which will lead you up on to the road itself.

Position 9. The Traditional Site

For many years, Ambion Hill was said not only to be the campsite of Richard, but also where the battle was fought. That said, there is little archaeological evidence to support either 1485 event. What has been found does, however, indicate that the Romans at least were here. There is good evidence for a Roman temple and a subsidiary manufacturing site seemingly specialising in a number of small 'horse and rider' brooches – which were, at least in some cases, subsequently offered to their gods at this temple site. There is also some evidence to suggest a Roman villa may well be located nearby.

Position 10. Richard's Mass

The Church of St James at Sutton Cheney is a Grade II listed building principally dating from the early thirteenth century. There has been some Victorian restoration work, but this has made little impact on the essential character of the church.

Sutton Cheney has only been an independent parish for a very short period of its history. Until 1882, it was a part of the parish of Market Bosworth, and its church a chapel of ease, daughter church of St Peter's in Market Bosworth. However, in the nineteenth century there was a great increase in the area of the village of Sutton Cheney, with industry thriving alongside agriculture. In consequence, from 1882 until 1923, Sutton Cheney had a period of prosperous independence – until it was again linked, not as a daughter church this time, but as an equal partner with the parish of Cadeby.

Since at least Victorian times, St James's Church has been said to have been used by Richard himself on the eve of the battle, however, it most likely that he would have heard Mass in his tent by one of his personal clergy. Indeed, his personal

The interpretation for Richard's camp.

prayer book, which is now in the collection at Lambeth Palace, was reputedly found in his tent after the battle. More likely some of Richard's men would have made their way here either to attend a service or simply to take private prayer and offer their soul to God. This is also true of the smaller St Martin's Church at Stapleton (built in about 1300), which is less than 2.5km or 1.5 miles to the east.

Position 11. Richard's Camp

As you stand on the grass trackway between the two fields looking out towards the village of Stoke Golding, with its tall spire breaking the skyline, and the smaller village of Dadlington, immediately to the left, you can easily imagine Richard astride his magnificent destrier or war horse, called White Surrey, in front of all his troops on that Monday morning, looking out over nearly the same view. The main difference in 1485 was that there would have been very few hedges. He most likely would have also been on the road that had led him from Leicester (some 16km or 10 miles) behind him and overlooking the main Watling Street (now the A5 some 8km or 5 miles) in front of him – just to the right of the village of Stoke Golding.

The Interpretation for Richard's Camp

In that early morning and immediately behind him, and probably either side of the Roman road, would have been hundreds of tents with their campfires. This is not the case for the more traditional site of Ambion Hill – the western end of the ridge, where there is little or no fresh water and no military tactical or logical reason to use it as a camp.

Thousands of men would have been preparing for battle. Some applying ornate and expensive armour with the aid of their squires. The vast majority, however, were preparing to fight in the same clothes they had lain down in the night before when they had tried to grab a few hours' sleep before going into fight for their lords and masters. They were the poor common soldier, who only a few days or weeks before had been the poor lowly serf. His protection in the coming battle was not beautiful beaten steel, but guile, good fortune and his fellow serfs around him. Due to the fact that most of the people on the field that day were not dressed in metal, today we struggle to find any evidence of their presence at all.

Richard may well have even been able to look out across the landscape that night and observe the campfires of his enemy, Henry Tudor. He straddled the road that would lead him, his men and, most importantly, his heavy and undoubtedly cumbersome ordnance down off the ridge and into battle the following morning. A number of archaeological pieces have been found in this area which can be attributed to potential camp litter, including a gilded harness pendant.

At some point on the Monday morning Richard and all his forces marched west, down off the ridge and towards his enemy. The date was 22 August 1485 – and history was about to be changed for ever.

Position 12. The Alternative Ambion Hill

Before crossing the stream, and slightly to your left, you can see a farm. This is Bradshaw Farm. The field directly in front of the buildings as you look at it today was originally two fields. The tithe map for this area, dated 1835, lists those fields as 'Nether Bradshaw' and 'Over Bradshaw'. On the first edition of the Ordnance Survey map of the same year one can clearly see Ambion Hill marked in those same Bradshaw fields, 3km south-east of where it is stated to be today. Is this a cartographer's mistake or is this indeed the true site of Ambion Hill?

Position 12. Looking out from the footpath to Bradshaw Farm – the alternative Ambion Hill.

The Opening Salvoes

Starting point: Sutton Cheney Wharf
Distance: 2.1km

Carefully leave the wharf by walking down the road to the west via the road bridge crossing the canal, towards the villages of Dadlington and Stoke Golding.

Having started down the road, you are now walking parallel and to the right of the original line of the Roman road. Look towards the right as you go and in the pasture fields (permanent grass fields) you will be able to see good examples of the old medieval ridge and furrow. This was created by a serf and his ox repeatedly going up and down the same line with his plough year after year after year. **Position 13. Richard's Route to Battle**.

As you pass the modern property on the left, the ground falls away, before rising after the crossroads. This is due to the Victorian railway line and the now demolished bridge crossing the road. The line was built in 1873 to transport coal between Moira and Nuneaton. The line was closed in 1965 with the bridge being pulled down in the early 1980s. In 1973 the line between Shenton village and Shackerstone reopened as a heritage line.

Carefully pass through the dip and then, 200m after the crossroads, turn left at the stile and take the footpath north, away from the road. Follow the footpath passing Apple Orchard Farm on your left. Continue along the footpath until you reach the end of the hedge. Cross the next field following the path which will lead

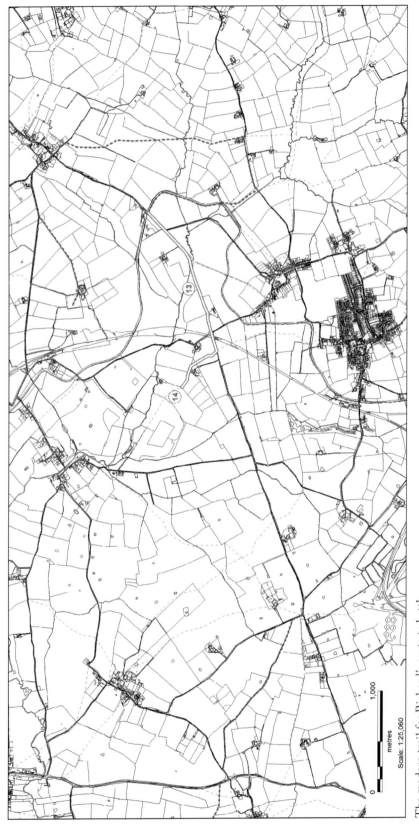

The modern trail for Richard's route to battle.

you to the far hedge diagonally to your right. As you cross, look further to your right and see the cottage at the end of the field. **Position 14. Mill Field**.

This is in the lowest ground around, and from a distance only the upper floor and roof can be seen. Look left and you see the ground reaching a rise before disappearing towards the west. The field you are crossing has been known for generations as Mill Field. You are also in the parish of Dadlington. What we do not know is if the mill that must have once stood somewhere near here was wind-powered or water-powered, for a stream still runs close to the cottage.

Position 13. Richard's Route to Battle

We have been able to create a map of the ridge and furrow in the immediate area. Traditional ploughs have the ploughshare and mouldboard on the right, and so turn the soil over to the right. This means that the plough cannot return along the same line for the next furrow. Instead, ploughing is done in a clockwise direction around a long rectangular strip (a *land*). After ploughing one of the long sides of the strip, the plough is removed from the ground at the end of the field, moved across the unploughed *headland* (the short end of the strip), then put back in the ground to work back down the other long side of the strip. The width of the ploughed strip is fairly narrow, to avoid having to drag the plough too far across the headland. This process has the effect of moving the soil in each half of the strip one furrow's width towards the centre line each time the field is ploughed.

In the Middle Ages each strip was managed by one family, within large open fields held in common (known as strip cultivation), and the locations of the strips were the same each year. The movement of soil year after year gradually built the centre of each strip up into a ridge, leaving a dip, or 'furrow', between each ridge (note that this use of 'furrow' is different from that for the small furrow left by each pass of the plough). The building up of a ridge was called *filling* or *gathering*, and was sometimes done before ploughing began. The raised ridges offered better drainage in a wet climate. Moisture drained into the furrows, and since the ridges were laid down a slope, in a sloping field water would collect in a ditch at the bottom. Only on some well-drained soils were the fields left flat. In damper soil, towards the base of the ridge, pulses (peas or beans) or dredge (a mixture of oats and barley) might be sown where wheat would have become waterlogged, as Thomas Tusser suggested in the sixteenth century:

> For wheat till land
> Where water doth stand.
> Sow pease or dredge
> below in that redge.

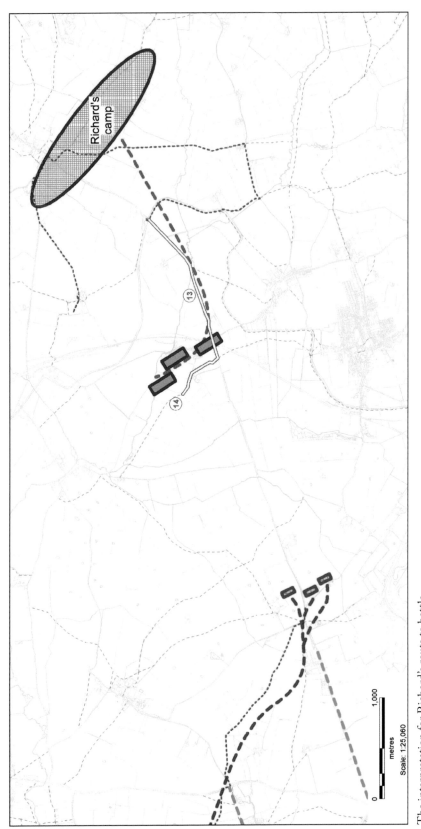

The interpretation for Richard's route to battle.

Individual plots were often demarcated by an obvious dip or gully. The strips would normally be a furlong – or furrow-long. That today equates to approximately 200m. The strip would vary in width from about 4.5m up to approximately 20m – the equivalent of a chain. This would result in an area ranging from 0.25 to 1 acre (0.1 to 0.4ha). Once an area had been ploughed, it would continue over centuries. Ridge and furrow would have been a common sight until the introduction of first steam ploughing in the 1800s and then the even greater revolutionary reversible plough in the 1950s. However, in some cases the old, original ridge and furrow fields were allowed to go to grass, and where this has been preserved it can still be seen today. The difference in height between the top of the ridge and the bottom of the furrow can be as great as 18 to 24in (0.5 to 0.6m) and the slowly inverted arching S can be clearly seen – especially in low, slanting light or with a good frost in the early morning.

The issue we have with the immediate landscape around the area of the battle is we do not know what ground was actively being farmed at the time and what had been left to turn to pasture. After the Black Death hit the Midlands in and around summer 1349 the population was decimated. The demand for crops – let alone the manpower to produce those crops – would have been hugely reduced. Vast swathes of land that had been under the plough only seasons ago were now no longer ploughed. As you walk around the landscape today, some of the land seen would have been under crop while some would have been undulating pasture.

Position 14. Mill Field

The modern-day road you have just been walking down runs adjacent to and slightly to the right of the line of the old Roman road. On the morning of Monday, 22 August 1485, Richard, possibly at the head of his army, would have marched along that same route. The army would have been possibly fifteen to twenty abreast, with banners unfurled preparing to go into battle.

As you take the footpath away from the road and the village of Dadlington, you are actually still within the ancient parish of Dadlington. The current footpath (or the road running parallel to the path) may well have been the ancient trackway leading to Dadlington Mill. I believe that this is also near to where Richard turned off the main route and took the route towards the mill.

As you walk along the path and past the farm that is today called Apple Orchard, but was once called 'Philadelphia' with a possible (but not proven) link to the Pilgrim Fathers, you will notice that the land both to the west and the east drops away. This is not a massive ridge running down from the south and Dadlington village, but if Richard was to the left, and Henry way off to the right, it would be enough to potentially hide the vast majority of Richard's army, while it changed from its travelling formation to the more aggressive battle formations.

The view looking west towards Henry's lines. This is the position where Richard may well have drawn up his guns.

As I have already tried to suggest, I think Richard had a master plan. Once he and his men were ready he brought his gun up onto the ridge that you are now walking along. For years the landowners have called this field 'Mill Field'. The windmill is mentioned in an agreement concerning tithes in Dadlington made in 1479. It was described as a new windmill in the lordship. The windmill was demolished in the sixteenth century, with a chancery document dating from the reign of Elizabeth I revealing that by the 1570s the mill had been 'taken down and sold to divers persons unknown the timbers and stones of the said mill by Robert Holte of Mancetter and his wife Katherine'. The land at that point was owned by Lord Ferrers of Chartley.

Norfolk was initially possibly somewhere near to North Farm, a couple of hundred yards to your right. Meanwhile, the guns start to open up. The battle has begun.

The Death of Norfolk

Starting point: From the end of The Opening Salvoes
Distance: 3.6km

Continue on the footpath from Apple Orchard Farm in a northerly direction, past the small footbridge leading to the barns off to your right and skirting the woods on your left. Follow this path ultimately to the road called Shenton Lane. **Position 15. Norfolk's Route to and from the Oxford Clash.**

Take this road to your right for about 200m before re-joining the footpath on the left-hand side of the road. (If you would like a comfort break or a snack, carry on along the road for a further 200m to Whitemoors Antiques Centre.) Once on the path, follow the left-hand hedge line to the end of the small field. Continue on into the second larger field keeping the stream to your left until you meet a yellow waymarker post, and pass through the hedge, over the stream and into another large

The modern trail for the Oxford/Norfolk clash.

metres

Scale: 1:25,060

0   1,000

field. Continue following the footpath through this field and then the adjoining one until you cross a ditch into yet another field. You are now travelling due south. Once you have crossed this field you enter the last big field before reaching the Fenn Lane road. **Position 16. Norfolk/Oxford Clash.**

To cross this last field, start to follow the footpath diagonally across towards the hedge on the opposite side of the field. Halfway across the field turn left and this second path takes you down the field to a stile about halfway between a pair of double gates and the left corner of the field.

Position 15. Norfolk's Route to and from the Oxford Clash

Norfolk was positioned on his lord's right flank. Once Richard had ordered some of his troops (and most importantly – his gun) to show themselves on the ridge, Norfolk and his battalia moved off; probably initially following the low-lying ground before reaching the footpath we see today as it crosses the modern road in front of you.

After the opening clash with Oxford, it is unclear if Norfolk made his way back to the 'relative' safety of the mill, or the lower lying ground behind the ridge, or was driven back as far as the mill. Either way, we are told by the early accounts that Norfolk died near a windmill.

Position 16. Norfolk/Oxford Clash

Henry and his commanders (and his men) would have been able to see Norfolk and his men, with their banners unfurled and flying in the breeze, marching out in a direction that might initially have seemed to have been away from them. However, it would have soon become apparent that they were in fact moving in a huge arc which, if not countered, would result in them being hit in the side.

Henry had to react, and both quickly and positively. Oxford and his battalia were sent out to engage the enemy. The quickest way for Oxford to do this was to move his men along the road in an easterly direction before turning nearly 90 degrees left, in a northerly direction. This manoeuvre both put the sun behind Oxford and a marshy area of ground to his right flank. It was around this point that the two battalias met in the first hand-to-hand fighting of the battle.

Oxford's numbers and, for that matter, Norfolk's are unknown for certain. However, we are led to believe that Norfolk had the superior numbers. To counter this Oxford tells his men to deploy themselves into a series of triangular configurations, or wedges. This was originally a Roman formation and Oxford ordered that his men should not move more than 10ft from their banners, thus creating a number of impenetrable blocks. Norfolk failed to break this simple but effective formation, and one can only guess at the injuries sustained on both sides

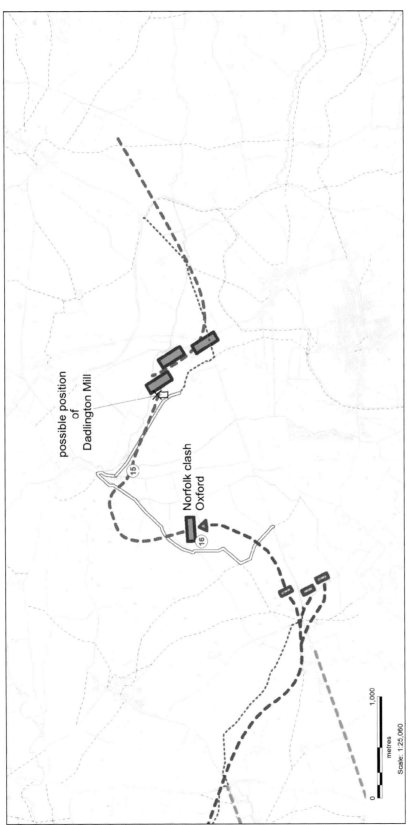

The interpretation of the Oxford/Norfolk clash.

as this melee moved slowly one way then the next as Norfolk tried to push home his attack, only to be parried by Oxford. During this fierce fighting both armies would be forced to stop due to the sheer exhaustion and dehydration. At some point John Howard, the First Duke of Norfolk was hit in the face with an arrow. Had he lost his helmet in the previous fighting – or had he simply lifted it momentarily from his head to get some fresh air and an astute Lancastrian spotting an opportunity loosed off an arrow, more in hope than expectation? Either way, Norfolk was mortally wounded and retreated back to the mill, where he finally succumbed to his wounds.

Oxford and his troops had successfully managed to hold their ground. However, they had left their leader more exposed.

Richard's Charge

Starting point: Footpath off Fenn Lane
Distance: 0.5km

Carefully cross Fenn Lane and make your way over the stile. Continue to walk along the footpath across the field until you reach the grass airstrip. Pause and look down the airstrip to your left (away from the farm buildings). **Position 17. The Start of Richard's Charge.**

Cross the airstrip and re-join the footpath across the field towards a corner of the field. Use the footbridge to go over the stream and then turn right to exit the field and join the road, Foxcovert Lane. **Position 18. The End of Richard's Charge.**

Position 17. The Start of Richard's Charge
Richard had carefully planned his battle strategy at least the night before, and though I am sure the intention was not to lose his leading commander in those early melees with Oxford, he had at least attained his first goal. One-third of Henry's forces had effectively left their leader. Richard could now set in motion the second part of his scheme.

As you look out, away from the farm behind you, the ground can be seen to rise gently. This is the ridge that Richard used to hide his manoeuvrings and get his troops ready to this time engage directly with Henry. His cavalry would have mounted the ridge possibly still at a controlled walk, for they would have been knee to knee, shoulder to shoulder – a solid mass of well-trained horse and steel below and expectant knight in steel on top. Flags unfurled, and with Richard leading from the front, this controlled body of men started to move down the gentle incline and in towards the enemy.

The charge had started – there was no going back!

The modern trail for Richard's final charge.

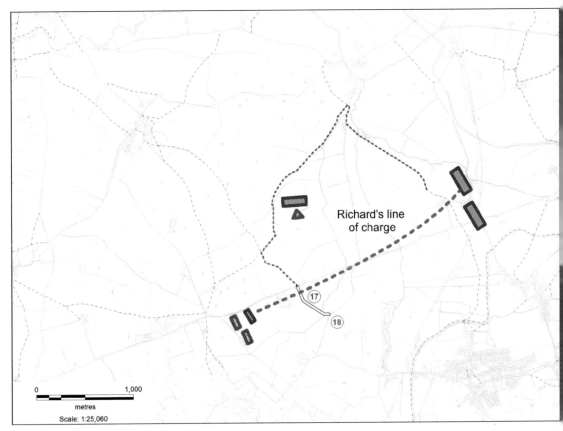

The interpretation of Richard's final charge.

Position 18. The End of Richard's Charge

From this position looking back from where you have walked Richard's charge went from your right to left. Probably straight through where the farm stands today. By the time Richard gets to that position he is probably less than 500m from Henry, and this is also when he might finally ask his destrier to charge. From the ridge to your right to Richard hitting Henry would take 4 minutes – just 240 seconds! That is less than the time it will take you to walk to the next road junction.

Stanley's Opportunity

Starting point: Foxcovert Lane
Distance: 2.1km

As you leave the field turn right and walk along the road for 400m to the T-junction. Turn left and walk for approximately 150m before pausing at the first large bend in the road. **Position 19. Stanley's Vantage Point.**

The modern trail for Stanley's route to battle.

Retrace your steps, back past the junction and follow the road past Foxcovert Farm. At the next junction turn right and follow the road for 1km back towards Fenn Lane. Once you have passed the house on your left, look right across the field to Fenn Lane Farm. **Position 20. Stanley Joins Henry.**

Continue on towards Fenn Lane, pausing at the gateway to the field on your left. **Position 21. The Line of Drive.**

Position 19. Stanley's Vantage Point

We are told by Polydore Vergil that Stanley 'stood betwixt the two armies, overlooking the field'. You are now standing near where I think Stanley sat astride his mount, watching the battle unfold in front of him. Next to him, and deliberately, was his foot. Stood in full view of both armies. And causing Lord Percy to have his men facing him to protect his king's flank as a precaution against attack. However, and more importantly, Stanley held his mounted force back behind the ridge and out of sight of Richard.

Behind you are the fields still known today by some locals as 'The Dining Table'. This where I propose that Stanley placed his camp. However, from in front of you Stanley would have been able to sit astride his horse and view the plain laid out in front. From here he would have seen the arrival of the two main protagonists and their troops. From here he would have heard the gun open up for Richard, then seen the flash and smelt that distinctive aroma of rotten eggs. But, most importantly, from here he would have seen Richard preparing for that infamous charge. He had to make a decision, and he had to make it now.

Position 20. Stanley Joins Henry

Stanley would have seen, far better than Henry, that Richard was about to execute a charge against the Welshman. He would be able to see from this raised vantage point that Richard was pulling his mounted knights around him, and then that they started, albeit at a controlled walk, then trot, that charge.

Stanley now had to make that choice. Did he stand (and face the consequences after the battle) or did he commit (and risk his life)? Of course – he committed. He was always going to fight. The question was, on whose side was he going to commit? He would have turned his horse, called his mounted troops to his side and made all reasonable speed towards the west – running in parallel but in front of Richard. The most important part of this manoeuvre was to keep behind the ridge. He needed to maintain the element of surprise for as long as he could. He needed his eventual arrival on the true battlefield to be a surprise to as many people as possible for as long as possible. The outcome of the battle depended on it.

Stanley and his mounted support would have followed a similar route to the one the modern road takes today. They would have covered approximately 2.5km, and assuming he undertook this at a canter (approximately 20kph), it would take him exactly 7½ minutes to reach Henry. A clear 90 seconds quicker than Richard hitting Henry – or at least Sir William Brandon, Henry's banner bearer, and then again before Richard went on to unseat Sir John Cheney. For Richard missed his opportunity of winning the battle – as he missed hitting the one man on the field which would have finished the fight and left Richard the king. Henry was still alive!

Position 21. The Line of Drive

We know that Stanley must have come from the west, due to the direction that Richard was driven back. If Stanley had come in on Henry's side and against Richard using the shortest route possible from his starting position, Richard would have been driven towards the north-west. Likewise, if he had come in from the south, Richard would have been pushed north.

From where you stand today we can accurately surmise that the initial contact between Henry and Richard was somewhere close to the small dew pond and clump of trees in the field immediately to your right and running alongside current Fenn Lane. We know that from one specific, small archaeological find, collected from the field in 2010 – a section of cross-guard.

This piece of cross-guard is fascinating. We know it is from a high-status sword. This is because it has an intricate design and is gilded. However, something that makes it more interesting is that it is made of bronze (or more accurately copper alloy). A cross-guard's primary function is to protect the user's hand and fingers from an opponent's blade, especially when it is being parried, i.e. blade on blade. A cross-guard therefore needs to be strong and be able to take the full force of an opponent's swinging blade – a blade that can easily break bones. A cross-guard was not only used in a defensive manner but in an offensive way. The sword could be held by the handle with one hand and the blade in the other. The end of the cross-guard could then be used to hit an opponent in the face. This was often used when in a melee, where it was sometimes so compressed that wielding a long sword effectively was difficult if not impossible. A third use of a cross-guard was to grab the blade in two hands and use the guard to literally hook your opponent and pull him off balance.

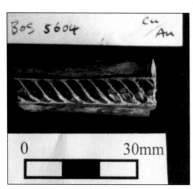

Part of a cross-guard. This is from a high-status sword and is made from bronze and gilded.

For any of these uses to work, the cross-guard needs to be strong and not be prone to breaking. It is normally, therefore, made of steel. However, in this case the cross-guard fragment is made of copper alloy which is intrinsically brittle. Why

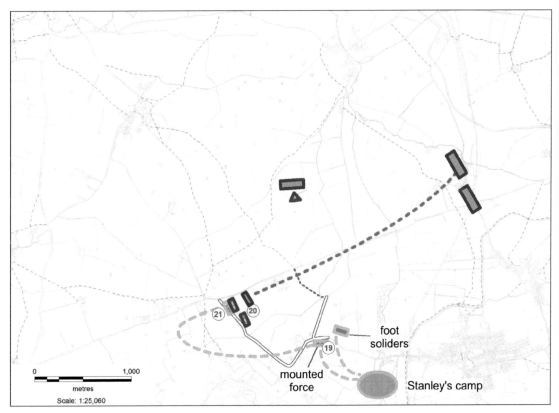

The interpretation of Stanley's route to battle.

would anyone choose to go into battle with a weapon that was potentially not safe? More importantly, who would go into battle with such a weapon? The answer must be a person of wealth, indeed probably extreme wealth given that it is gilded; but also, someone whose chosen weapons did not include a sword – or at least not that sword. This sword must have been for show or possibly ceremonial. His chosen weapons were potentially the lance and a war hammer (or mace). I would not dare to suggest that this was part of Richard's personal armoury, but I do think that it may have been owned by someone involved in that initial hit between Richard's charging knights and those immediately surrounding Henry. Other finds in this immediate area include a buckle, a harness pendant, two strap fittings, a badge or mount and a spur rowel.

We now know where that initial hit took place – seconds before Stanley joined Henry. We also know where that drive finished – 600m and nearly due east at the marsh, near where the 'Bosworth Boar' was found. It is therefore a simple task of projecting back in a straight(ish) line to work out where Stanley must have come from.

Percy, Earl of Northumberland

Starting point: Fenn Lane
Distance: 1.5km

On regaining Fenn Lane, turn right and carefully follow the road, past Fenn Lane Farm. Pause at the double gates on your right which you will find about 300m past the farm. **Position 22. The Marsh.**

Continue for another 500m along Fenn Lane to the junction on your right. **Position 23. Percy's Options and Richard's Death.**

Position 22. The Marsh
A lot of people's perception of a marsh is a large expanse of liquid mud, an impenetrable area, that once entered, no one will come out of. The area here was probably considerably safer – at least for the locals and individuals, with only small areas of exposed water. However, there would have been sedge and other similar marginal plants growing over a large area (and these still grow here today).

A local serf probably would have been able to negotiate both himself and his one cow without getting muddy. However, from a commander's point of view, and especially a 'non-local' one, there would have been areas of ground (and on both sides of the road) that he would have tried to avoid – especially with a large body of men in any form of organised, manageable formation.

However, it was to the area immediately south of the road that Stanley and Henry drove what remained of Richard's mounted troop from their initial contact, approximately 600m to the west.

Position 23. Percy's Options and Richard's Death
Percy led Richard's third battalia, positioned on the left of Richard and probably to the south of the road. His main function was to protect his liege's flank from any enemy assault. From the start of the battle, the main enemy was Henry Tudor, however, there was still a perceived enemy in Stanley, standing on the rising ground to the south-west. Who was Stanley going to fight for and, more importantly, who was he going to fight against?

Richard could not afford to ignore Stanley, as an attack on his unprotected left flank could be fatal. Henry Percy, 4th Earl of Northumberland was put facing Stanley, to protect the left flank if Stanley attacked. Stanley' foot soldiers could be seen on the rise – possibly even Stanley himself might have been made out, on his mount, walking up the ranks, talking to his knights, watching the enemy. Watching Richard. Watching Percy.

During the battle things changed. Norfolk, the leader of the king's right flank, moved out away from the main body, out towards the north. Oxford, from the rebel

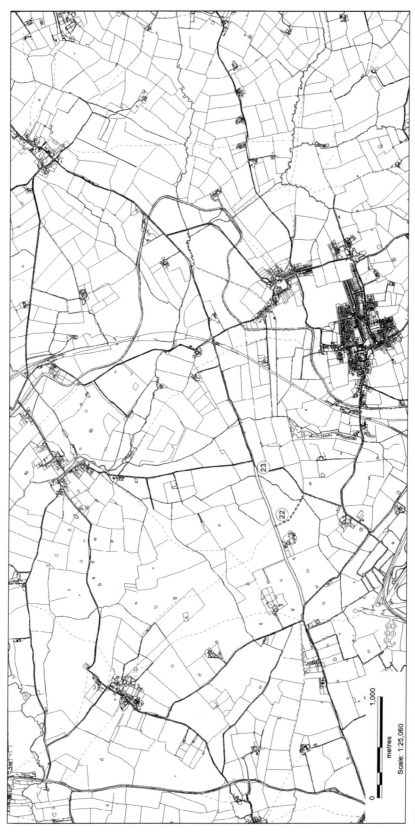

The modern trail for the death of Richard.

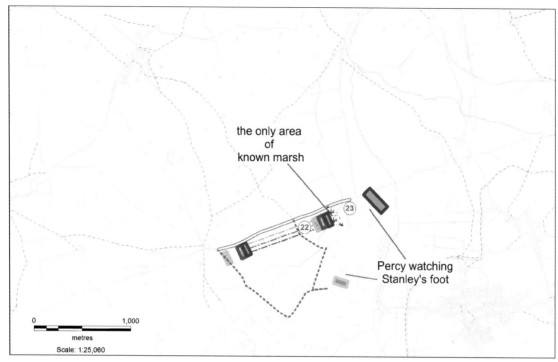

the only area
of
known marsh

Percy watching
Stanley's foot

0   1,000
metres
Scale: 1:25,060

The interpretation of the death of Richard.

army, moved out to meet him. From his position, Percy would be able to see the ensuing melee. However, it is unlikely that he would be able to see Norfolk getting mortally wounded. What Percy would have seen undoubtedly, and I would suggest certainly knew was going to happen the day before, was Richard leading a body of men out from behind the rise and out across the plain, passing Percy from behind him and on his right flank.

Percy would then have been able to watch Richard move from a controlled walk, through trot and canter and finally into a headlong charge towards his adversary, Henry. Through this process Percy would have had half an eye on the Stanley troops, who continued to stand, and stand facing Percy's battalia. Percy therefore was probably the most surprised of everyone when just after Richard met Henry – Stanley pops up behind Henry, on horse and with fresh troops. Not only that, but Richard is forced back.

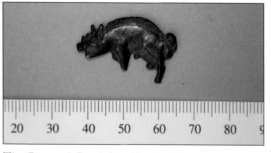

The 'Bosworth Boar', found by Carl Dawson on 9 September 2009. It is a small find – but one of major significance in the interpretation of the Battle of Bosworth.

Suddenly their plan of the night before starts to unravel. What can Percy do? He needs time to think. What is Stanley's foot doing on the ridge? They are still where they have been the whole battle – they do not look like they are doing anything. Can he turn his troops to go and move to support his king? If he does that, he will have to avoid the marsh that lies between him and Richard. He must support his king, his friend. He wants to.

However, now Richard is in the marsh. Richard is unseated from his mount. Percy cannot see him anymore for the enemy surrounding his king. The fighting has stopped. What has happened? Richard is dead. The battle is over – the battle is lost!

The Crowning of Henry Tudor

Starting point: The junction of Fenn Lane and Foxcovert Lane
Distance: 0.6km

Take the junction off Fenn Lane and walk back up Foxcovert Lane, to the footpath used earlier. Pause for a second time. **Position 24. The Crowning of Henry.**

Position 24. The Crowning of Henry

With the death of Richard, Henry was now automatically king. The Tudor Dynasty had begun. The formal coronation was held in Westminster Abbey, but not for another eight weeks, on 30 October 1485. However, to show to his men – and his enemies, that he was the victor, and indeed that Richard was dead, he was crowned on the field in front of all. To add weight to the fact that he was the 'rightful and true king' this crowning took place (all be it allegedly) with the very diadem that had been around the head of Richard.

So that as many people as possible could witness this momentous event, Henry was crowned near to where the majority of men were still standing, where a few moments before they had been trying to kill each other. According to the 'Ballad of Bosworth Field', it was to 'a mountayne hyghe'. Holinshed states Henry went to 'the top of a littell mountaine'. More recently some people put the actual crowning at or very near the current site of Crown Hill Farm. I suspect though that it was not a 'hyghe' place but a dry place. In other words, up the nearest slope out of the marsh, out of the wet, out of the blood and gore of battle. The slope you are now looking down – towards where we now know today there was a medieval marsh, and where we found the small broken but beautiful 'Bosworth Boar', was the most likely place for this impromptu people's coronation. Before the battle, this was part of an area known as Garbrodfelde. Since the battle the name changed and became known as part of the great field of Crown Hill Field. More importantly, it was given this name at some point between 1467/8 and 1605.

The modern trail for the crowning of Henry VII.

Scale: 1:25,070

metres

0   1,000

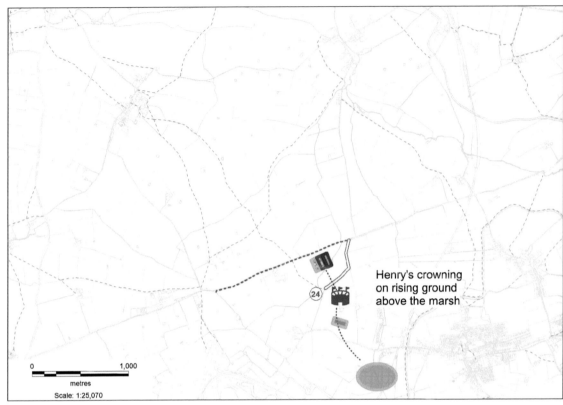

Henry's crowning
on rising ground
above the marsh

0   1,000
metres
Scale: 1:25,070

The interpretation of the crowning of Henry VII.

Crown Hill

Starting point: Foxcovert Lane
Distance: 1.6km

From the footpath carry on along Foxcovert Lane to the main junction. Turn left on to Upton Lane, past Stanley's position and walk on into the village of Stoke Golding. Cross the Ashby Canal again and start making your way up the hill. Pause at the farm on the left. **Position 25. Crown Hill Farm.**

Position 25. Crown Hill Farm
Crown Hill Farm today lies on the western edge of the village of Stoke Golding. It is a fairly modern building, although we know there was a farm here at least 130-odd years ago in 1897. What we do not know is if there was anything here 530-odd years ago.

If you walk less than 200m further along the road one can see a blue plaque. Erected in 2000 by the local Charity of Thomas Barton, it suggests that the crowning was in fact nearer still to the middle of the village – and the church.

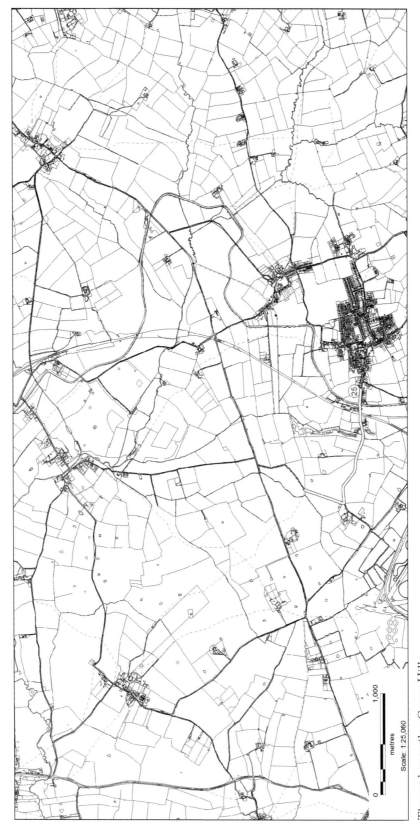

The modern trail to Crown Hill.

Stoke Golding Church

Starting point: Crown Hill Farm, Station Road, Stoke Golding
Distance: 0.6km

Carry on along Station Road into the village of Stoke Golding. When you reach the George and Dragon Public House, take the left junction, called the High Street, and continue past the Three Horseshoes and follow the road round a tight left-hand bend. Continue for less than 75m and turn left again along Church Walk to the Church of St Margaret of Antioch. **Position 26. Stoke Golding Church.**

   This church is a Grade I listed building that dates back to the Saxon period. Sir Nikolaus Bernhard Leon Pevsner CBE FBA, a German-British art and architectural historian best known for his monumental forty-six-volume series of county-by-county guides, *The Buildings of England*, described it as 'one of the most beautiful churches in Leicester'. There is an impressive openwork quatrefoil parapet on the south wall which is matched by the parapet at the top of the tower, which includes renditions of the heads of King Edward III and Queen Philippa on the south face. The tower has been a landmark in the surroundings for many years. However, it was in fact taken down during the Second World War due to its proximity to nearby Lindley aerodrome. Each stone was laboriously numbered so they could be reassembled at the conclusion of the war.

   Inside the church, the arcade between the nave and aisle makes an imposing feature. This succession of contiguous arches are supported by a colonnade of shafted and filleted columns or piers and dates from the early fourteenth century. There are moulded arches and carved capitals with foliage and heads, including ladies wearing wimples, a youth with signs of toothache and two 'green men'. The south aisle and adjoining chapel contain two piscinae. The purpose of the piscina, or sacrarium, is to dispose of water used sacramentally, by returning these particles directly to the earth. For this reason it is connected by a pipe directly to the ground. The wall features remnants of fourteenth-century paintings. The font dates from about 1330 and shows carved representations of St Nicholas, St Katharine and St Margaret, as well as heraldic panels.

   St Margaret was known as St Margaret of Antioch in the West and as St Marina the Great Martyr in the East. She is said to have been martyred in 304, but this was declared apocryphal by Pope Gelasius I in 494, although devotion to her revived in the West with the Crusades. She was reputed to have promised very powerful indulgences to those who wrote or read her life, or invoked her intercessions; these no doubt helped the spread of her *cultus*. Margaret is one of the Fourteen Holy Helpers, and is one of the saints Joan of Arc claimed to have spoken with. According to the version of the story in *The Golden Legend*, she was a native of Antioch and the daughter of a pagan priest named Aedesius. Her mother having died soon after her birth, Margaret was nursed by a Christian woman 5 or 6 leagues (6.9–8.3 miles) from Antioch. Having embraced Christianity and consecrated her virginity to God, Margaret was disowned by her father, adopted by her nurse and lived in the country keeping sheep with her foster mother (in what is now Turkey). Olybrius, Governor of the Roman Diocese of the East, asked her to marry him, but with the demand that she renounce Christianity. Upon her refusal, she was cruelly tortured, during which various miraculous incidents occurred. One of these involved being swallowed by Satan in the shape of a dragon, from which she escaped alive when the cross she carried irritated the dragon's innards.

St Margaret of Antioch. An illustration in her hagiography depicting her beating a demon with a hammer, printed in Greece, dated 1858.

Position 26. Stoke Golding Church

Stoke Golding's unique historical claim to fame is that in 1485 the people of the village witnessed the unofficial 'rural coronation' of Henry VII. In so doing Stoke Golding claims to be the 'Birthplace of the Tudor Dynasty'.

Traditional local accounts tell of the villagers climbing on to the battlements of the Church of St Margaret of Antioch to view the bloody battle on 22 August 1485. Indeed, from the tower, the site of the battle would have been easily visible as it is only 1½km to the north-west and you would have been able to hear someone from the top of the roof shouting down to the rest of the villagers a blow-by-blow account of what was happening.

Stoke Golding church.

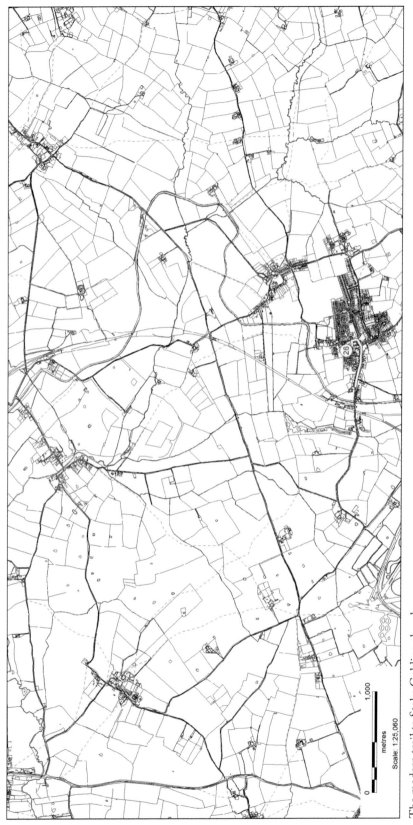

The modern trail to Stoke Golding church.

Another local tradition is based around the windowsills of the church, as they show grooves which legend has it were caused by the soldiers sharpening their swords and axes on the eve of the battle. However, it is more likely that these were the result of many years of the local graveyard maintenance team sharpening their scythes in preparation for cutting the grass.

Dadlington Church

Starting point: Stoke Golding Church
Distance: 1.3km

Leave Stoke Golding church and return to the main road. Turn left and follow the road past the White Swan Public House and the Zion Baptist Church. Follow the road past the farm and down the hill to the small moorings on the Ashby de la Zouch Canal. Carry on up the hill and approximately 250m from the canal you will see a footpath on your left through the hedge and into a small paddock. Cross the stile and take this path up through the field. Cross two more stiles and arrive at the green in the village of Dadlington. Turn left again and follow the road to the small Church of St James the Greater, 100m in front of you. **Position 27. Dadlington Church.**

The Parish Church of St James the Greater was built some time before 1283 and is dedicated to James, son of Zebedee, who was one of the Twelve Apostles of Jesus. In 1889 William Winter, in his book *Gray Days and Gold in England and Scotland*, wrote about the church in a scathing way:

> Dadlington church has almost crumbled to pieces, but it will be restored. It is a diminutive structure, with a wooden tower, stuccoed walls, and a tiled roof, and it stands in a graveyard full of scattered mounds and slate-stone monuments. It was built in Norman times, and although still used it has long been little better than a ruin. One of the bells in its tower is marked 'Thomas Arnold fecit, 1763'. The church contains two pointed arches, and across its nave are five massive oak beams, almost black with age. The plaster ceiling has fallen, in several places, so that patches of laths are visible in the roof. The pews are square, box-like structures, made of oak and very old. The altar is a plain oak table, supported on carved legs, covered with a cloth. On the west wall appears a tablet, inscribed, 'Thomas Eames, church-warden, 1773'. Many human skeletons, arranged in regular tiers, were found in Dadlington churchyard, when a revered clergyman, the Rev Mr Bourne, was buried, in 1881, and it is believed that those are remains of men who fell at Bosworth Field.

In 1890 major restoration of the church was carried out under the then vicar, the Revd Henry Lomax. The outside was re-stuccoed and the bell tower was also fully restored.

As a resident of the village – and someone who looks over the battle site on a daily basis, I have often wondered what I would have done as a man of the village in 1485 with armies coming at me from all directions? Could I hide in the hayricks? What was going to happen to my wife and daughter? Would the village be pillaged? Could I make some money out of this once it was all over? There could be easy pickings off the dead.

From many accounts a large number of the dead were carried to Dadlington and buried in the churchyard; in 1886, for example, the *Leicester Chronicle* reported that 'skeletons and broken fragments of rusty armour still frequently obstruct the peasant's plough, and the old churchyard has known many ghastly re-interments of the poor soldiers remains'. In 1511 Henry VIII issued a warrant for prayers to be said for those 'slayn' in the battle'. A Letter of Confraternity specifies praying at St James's Chapel for the souls of bodies of men slain, brought and buried. Prayers are still said in the church on the Sunday nearest to 22 August to remember those who died. In 1622, local historian William Burton described the 'chapel dedicated to Saint James is in the churchyard whereof many of the dead bodies (slain in the said battaile) was buried'. County historian John Nichols, in 1782 and 1811, referred to burials and indented spaces in the graveyard. Later, there were reports of the discovery of 'compacted masses of human bones' in the churchyard in 1868, *c.* 1900 and 1950.

Dadlington church – looking from the north.

The modern trail to Dadlington church.

Position 27. Dadlington Church

As with St Margaret's Church in Stoke Golding, St James's Church in Dadlington was built before the time of the battle. Therefore, people from the village may well have stood round the church to watch the proceedings. This would have included on the Sunday evening and watching the campfires of Richard's men flickering in the moonlight. As a man of the village what was I thinking? Was I going to press-ganged into fighting tomorrow?

Return to the Battlefield Heritage Centre

Starting point: Dadlington Church
Distance: 3km

Leave Dadlington church and turn right past the Dog and Hedgehog Public House. Carefully cross the road, and the stile opposite the junction. You have now entered a field known locally as the 'Balis 'ole'. This field was excavated for sand and gravel used in the construction of the railway and canal.

Follow the footpath over the next stile and turn right and then cross the third stile. At this point follow the dedicated footpath, which is straight on, keeping to the left of the hedge which is in front of you. Cross the canal, using the farm bridge, and make your way down to the road. Once at the road, turn right and carefully follow the road over the canal to Sutton Cheney Wharf. Enter Sutton Wharf and pass the cafe and toilets, picking up the footpath that runs parallel to the canal. Follow this footpath through the adjoining field and then on into the wood. Once in Ambion Wood follow the footpath until you make your way back to the Bosworth Battlefield Heritage Centre.

Congratulations – you have now completed the self-guided tour of the battlefield.

The modern trail back to the battlefield heritage centre.

Chapter 17

Areas for Future Research

'History is fact – it is only our interpretation that keeps changing.'

A t the beginning of this book, I stated that it has been written to encourage all who read it to question what has gone before, to enter into a discussion with an open mind and to set aside preconceived ideas. Therefore, I am not trying to say that everything I have written is correct – only time will tell. Time, when more research can and must be undertaken. Where the various hypothesizes touched on in these pages can be tested and proven – or not as the case may be. Along with other theories from other historians, academics and indeed people who have no direct interest in Richard, Henry, Bosworth or even the medieval period in general – but have that interest and knowledge in something that when put into that cauldron and simmered for a while the truth will eventually come to the top.

> If everything else is found to be unlikely,
> what is left must be the most likely.

We have not finished researching Bosworth. Indeed, we probably never will. However, where things will go, what new technologies will become available and how things will move on – who knows. But I suspect it will be an interesting ride!

It was quickly realised before we even started to locate the true site of the battlefield that the metal-detectorists needed to change their methodology, and rather than wandering around a field, they were given a formal grid system and individual GPS monitoring equipment. Initially the grid pattern was 20m apart, but this was swiftly brought down to 10m intervals. After a couple of seasons this was reduced again to 5m intervals and ultimately regular detecting was based on 2.5m intervals. The members of AHARG have become the specialists in this systematic approach to metal-detecting. It is the only effective method of getting a clear picture of finds, while maintaining a reasonable speed across the landscape. Nearly all detecting was undertaken using a discrimination mode, i.e. not searching for all metals such as iron but limiting the finds to metal such as lead, copper alloy and precious metals. This was necessary to reduce the number of signals produced by modern farming debris, which would have significantly hampered the progress of the survey team. Though the project was looking for evidence of the battle – which took place over

2½ hours on that fateful Monday morning in 1485 – finds from other periods were collected and recorded on the project database.

In 2009, Leicestershire County Council and the Battlefields Trust were able to announce to the world that they were able to answer the question of where the Battle of Bosworth was fought. We had successfully found conclusive evidence, for at least part of the fighting, and possibly found evidence for Richard's camp and even potentially his rout. However, as with any type of similar project, in trying to answer one question, we had ended up with many more unanswered ones.

By 2011, most fieldwork, along with other research work, managed under the umbrella of Leicestershire County Council had effectively come to a halt. The research area amounted to an area of approximately 3,370 hectares (33.70km²). This went from the village of Sutton Cheney in the east to land either side of Fenn Lane, immediately adjacent to ground owned by Horiba MIRA Technology Park in the west. Though we had managed to locate some of the battlefield, we had also discovered evidence of other periods in history, and any future fieldwork in this area should continue to do so. Currently other periods of interest would include the newly discovered Roman areas near the Sundial and Fenn Lane, the potential Civil War scatter near the 'Bow Tie Field' and the scatter of four Neolithic stone axes along Fenn Lane.

Leicestershire County Council, along with the Battlefields Trust, instigated a major part of the research into the Battle of Bosworth, especially with the help of the National Lottery Heritage Fund grant between 2004 and 2009. They answered the question posed by the Lottery of can you find a medieval battle site and locate (at least part) of the Battle of Bosworth in the landscape? However, AHARG as a team of volunteers started working on and around Ambion Hill as long ago as 1999, and still comes together to try and learn more about the historical aspects of the site through both archaeological and desktop research. As a founder member of AHARG I feel that this work should (and will) continue. Not just looking at those 2½ hours, but allowing both us and others who may be looking at other historical periods or specific events to use our data that now covers not only a huge period through time but a growing area of the landscape.

With respect to future work on the battle, we know that it was fought by three armies. These were led by King Richard III, Henry Tudor, Earl of Richmond, later known as Henry VII, and at least one of the Stanley brothers, Sir William Stanley with possible remote support from Thomas, Lord Stanley. Any research undertaken into the battle must include aspects of all sides, to try to understand not only who and where the fighting took place, but why did the fighting take place in a specific area. It should also try and locate evidence for any campsites and possible line of rout. Hypotheses can be tested and then accepted, tweaked or rejected.

Potential Future Projects

The following section is really no more than a set of bullet points (excuse the pun), and in no particular order, to suggest possible projects. Some of these, if taken up, may lead to dead ends or completely new projects and areas of research. It is by no means a definitive list. I would suggest that any person or group with a proposed project, based around either the 1485 Battle of Bosworth or anything else connected to the site within the proposed survey area, should submit a brief to the central body, ideally AHARG.

This does not mean that the projects have to have support or be sanctioned by the central body, but it should make other people aware of similar projects being undertaken, and therefore either allow for joint working or at least prevent duplication. With respect to any fieldwork, access to land should always be made via the central body. Any fieldwork is done with the blessing of the local landowners. Their best interests are, and must always be, paramount.

The categories have been divided into two main groups.

- Fieldwork – anything that might require access to the physical countryside, within the proposed research.
- Non-Fieldwork – any project that is fundamentally desk-based. The exception to this would potentially be any new interpretation of evidence (such as interpretation points or boards, or a new exhibition area for the Roman finds).

Fieldwork

Metal-Detecting

- Extend the metal detecting archaeological survey work in all directions using the 2.5m transect method, beyond our current area of known worked fields. This should allow us to accurately determine the extent of the actual battle site. This will then permit a more accurate designation for the Battlefield Registration. Thus, hopefully protecting all of the site for future generations.
- Re-metal-detect the 10m survey fields at 2.5m intervals, between the 'Fen Hole' and the 'Mill Field' scatters to ascertain if there are two distinct scatters or one far larger scatter.
- Re-metal-detect the areas where the original roundshot have been found, as we know from experience that not all evidence is captured at the first visit or in the same agricultural season.
- Undertake further metal-detecting near Sutton Cheney village to look for evidence of a possible Ricardian campsite.

5m gridded metal-detecting, which we now realise must be undertaken at 2.5m intervals.

- Undertake metal-detecting in fields around Merevale Abbey to see if there is any evidence for Henry Tudor's campsite.
- Undertake metal-detecting in fields around Sheepy to see if there is any more evidence for Henry Tudor's campsite.
- Undertake metal-detecting in fields around 'The Dining Table' to see if there is any evidence for a Stanley campsite, or post-battle resting of Henry's army.
- Undertake an 'all-metal' survey in key hotspot areas. These should include around some of the key finds such as the first cross guard and the nearby 'Bosworth Boar'. Is there evidence for the arrow storms? This is because ferrous objects represent 90 per cent of metalwork carried at the battle and include arrowheads – if they survive in the plough soil.

Environmental Work

- Find the full extent of the medieval marsh, by using a systematic survey approach starting at the area of known marsh – potentially at 2.5m intervals.
- Find the full extent of the Roman-Anglo-Saxon marsh (*c.* seventh century).
- Identify ancient hedgerows and field boundaries, in search of medieval enclosures.

Geophysical Surveying

- Undertake a geophysical survey of 'Mill Field' to try and ascertain the whereabouts and type of the Dadlington windmill, built *c.* 1479 – does this correlate with the finds?
- Undertake a geophysical survey of 'Battle Field' (opposite Whitemoors car park) looking for a possible grave pit.
- Undertake a geophysical survey of field immediately south of 'King Dick's Well' looking for a possible grave pit.
- Undertake a geophysical survey of earthworks on the Disused Medieval Village immediately east of 'King Dick's Well'. This will require specific permission.

Soil sampling with a handheld auger – looking for peat.

Undertaking a geophysical survey.

Excavation

- Undertake a test trench across the earthworks on DMV to ascertain period of habitation. (Possible Roman through to medieval – did it become redundant suddenly perhaps due to plague?) This will need specific permission.
- Undertake test trenches on any possible grave pits located within the landscape – and possible keyhole work in Dadlington churchyard.
- Undertake further test trenches in the Roman temple field, across potential field boundaries.

Non-Fieldwork

Computer Work

- Complete the database of all current finds. This must include images of all the finds.
- Have all of the probable and all of the possible battle finds re-analysed and compare them with finds from the Battle of Towton site and or the Royal Armouries. Update the database accordingly.
- Increase the LIDAR, or 'laser imaging, detection and ranging', coverage to include at least Upton and Lindley.
- Map all the 'human' features in the medieval landscape, such as trackways, roads, boundaries and buildings (from A447 near Sutton Cheney to Merevale).
- Create an accurate computer generated 3D terrain model. The model should at least be able to show viewsheds of the medieval landscape from certain key points based on an eye height of 5ft 8in and 7ft 8in (foot soldier and mounted knight) looking out over the landscape in specific directions as 'soldiers on foot and on horseback'. In other words, if someone was positioned at a certain point in the landscape, either on foot or on horseback, could they see the enemy if they were in specific parts of the landscape?

The primary use of the model is for researchers to more fully understand the subtleties of the landscape without the modern landscape features and tree cover. This will provide greater clarity as to how the local topography might have affected the routes taken by the armies, their campsite locations, their deployment positions and where and how they engaged with each other.

However, there are other uses such a model could be put to. With further investment, the model could be incorporated in the battlefield heritage centre exhibition as part of an animated film showing the 'current' battlefield theory. Or it could be the basis for a 'Bannockburn visitor centre'-style battle interactive, in which visitors can create their own version of the battle – Richard might even win!

With the appropriate GPS software and interface, the model could be used in the actual landscape on a laptop, mobile phone or other portable device, allowing the viewer to see now and then views of the area.

It could be viewed through the HoloLens system, either in the actual landscape or somewhere completely different in the world. These are currently being used across the construction industry to look at items in 'hyper reality'.

The model also has potential commercial use, as it could be sold to a gaming company as the basis for a 'Battle of Bosworth Wargame'.

- Identify all possible firing positions for guns (Richard, Henry or/and Stanley?) from LIDAR maps and 'line of site', as well as tested firing ranges. Explore any other international medieval cannon firing tests undertaken and compare results with the Cranfield University exercise. We know exactly where the collected roundshot were located, and we know that they will have been moved very little by ploughing or 'stone picking'. We also know that the gunners would have fired only at a target that they could physically see. Accurate mapping of the landscape should allow us, therefore, to at least rule out large areas of the landscape where the guns could not have been positioned leaving us with fewer options as to where they could have been.
- Complete and publish a database of as many men as possible who fought in battle.

Research Work

- Identify as many of the medieval field names for the ancient parishes between Merevale and Sheepy in the east and Fenn Lane Farm.
- Identify as many landowners as possible at or around the end of the medieval period. This should include land ownership prior to the battle, but also post-battle.
- What ground was owned by Merevale Abbey – was this a possible/probable Tudor campsite?
- Check holdings of Leicester Abbey, which held Garbrodys in 1470.
- Was any ground awarded to the victorious armies or to the Church, in thanks for support – or taken in retribution? There are at least six fields in Sutton Cheney owned by the 'Bishops of St David's' on the Enclosure map of 1794 which cover some 530-plus acres.
- Compile a history of 'Ambion DMV'. Where was it, how large and when did it die out? The village appears in records between 1271 and 1303 as Anebein or Hanebein. The last known reference is in 1346 and it may have been at

least partly depopulated by the plague a few years later and never reoccupied, then cleared by the landowner.

- Identify any/all possible sites of grave pits using 'verbal tradition' sources as well as written accounts.
- Compile and research the many and varying Bosworth traditions, published by Hutton, Nichols, Austin etc., as well as local oral traditions, which relate to finds, locations and theories.

Interpretation

- Keep all interested partners and the public at large informed of all new information as soon as appropriate, perhaps via a newsletter or social media, as well as an independent website.
- Interpret the most likely route that Richard may have taken from Leicester to the battle. Produce a walking or/and cycle leaflet and trail including all the relevant local sites.
- Interpret the possible route that Henry may have taken from South Wales to the battle. Produce a trail with walking or/and cycle leaflets.

The extent of the potential modelling area. A map showing a revised 8,000 hectares or 80km² potential research area with Richard's probable camp in the north-east; Henry's probable campsite in the north-west; Merevale Abbey in the west; Stanley's probable campsite in the south; and the clash of Richard and Henry at Fenn Lane Farm.

Potential Related Finds from the Portable Antiquities Scheme

T he list detailed in the table below has been extracted from the Portable Antiquities Scheme (PAS) for recorded finds which could be related to activities surrounding the skirmish on or around 21 August 1485 and the battle on 22 August 1485. PAS is run by the British Museum on behalf of the Museums, Libraries and Archives Council. There is a network of Finds Liaison Officers, often based in museums and county councils throughout England and Wales, and the data gathered by the scheme is published on an online database accessible to all (www.finds.org.uk). Most of the 7,000-plus finds from the research project are not on this database.

Old Find ID	Image	Object Type	Description
WMID-AEE185		DAGGER	A copper alloy dagger quillon of medieval date. The quillon is lozenge-shaped with four faceted edges, tapering towards the terminals. Each end terminates in a multi-faceted knop. The centre of the quillon has a sub-oval aperture through which the tang of the blade would originally have passed. The quillon has a grey patina in the centre which differs from the greener patina at either end, indicating that this would once have been covered, perhaps by leather which would have helped secure the tang in place. The quillon is slightly concave on one side, and slightly convex on the other. It measures 66.1mm long, 1.2mm wide, 5.1mm thick and weighs 13.4g.
LEIC-33AD61		SEAL MATRIX	Medieval copper alloy seal matrix, 17mm in diameter and 19mm long. The object is in fair condition with a green patina and weighs 5.61g. The object consists of a circular matrix which may feature an image of a

Old Find ID	Image	Object Type	Description
			bird? It has a sub-circular shaft which tapers from the reverse of the matrix and terminates with a protruding collar and a circular suspension loop. The inscription is too worn to make out.
LEIC-43E076		SEAL MATRIX	Medieval copper alloy seal matrix, 28mm long, 12mm wide and 2mm thick. The object is in fair condition, having worn edges, has a brown patina and weighs 5.17g. The matrix is a 'pointed oval' in form and is rectangular in section. It has a raised central rib which widens as it approaches the edge which contains a semi-circular protrusion 6mm deep and 10mm wide. The matrix is illustrated with a lamb holding a flag (Agnus Dei). The illustration appears to have Lombardic lettering, but it will need cleaning to make this legible.
LEIC-F5B594		SEAL MATRIX	Medieval lead-alloy seal matrix, 29mm in diameter. The matrix is circular and is fairly crudely made with a folded over strip of lead forming a handle. It has an unreadable inscribed border with a cross at the top. The central incised design is of a segmented wheel.
LEIC-4CA137		CHAPE	Medieval copper alloy sword chape, 52mm long, 34mm wide and 16mm deep. The object is in fair condition with a green/brown patina and weighs 26g. The chape is plain and triangular in form with an uneven, damaged upper edge. It terminates with a semi-spherical knop, 6mm in diameter.
SWYOR-9DE267		HARNESS PENDANT	A copper alloy shield-shaped harness pendant with heraldic decoration. It is shaped like a pointed shield with a suspension loop (set at right angles) at the top in the centre. The loop is broken. The front of the pendant was decorated with enamel and gilding, patches of which are still visible.

Old Find ID	Image	Object Type	Description
			Both the front and back have a light-green patina. The heraldic design comprises a red background with three gold lions passant and a blue label (band) at the top. The label has three rectangles (points) hanging down. The heraldic description is: Gules three lions passant guardant in pale or a label azure. These are the arms of England with a label of France and are those of the earls (and subsequently dukes) of Lancaster. The back of the pendant is rough but undecorated. It is medieval in date, probably fourteenth century. It measures 36.9mm long, 25.6mm wide, 7mm thick and weighs 6.32g. See also Record IDs DOR-DEFB74 and SUSS-8E0011 on the PAS database, https://finds.org.uk/.
LEIC-674A50		SEAL MATRIX	Medieval copper alloy seal matrix, 18mm long and 14mm in diameter. The object is in fair condition with a green patina and weighs 5.98g. The object consists of a hexagonal shaft, which is missing its loop. It widens to form a circular platform for the matrix. This is shield-shaped and its upper rectangular area contains an image of a mythical beast, perhaps a dragon or a mermaid? Below this is an anchor like motif made up of an upturned crescent sitting on a shaft which terminates in an open circle. The shaft has a short cross bar which appears to have a bird sitting on it. There are traces of an inscription, but it is very worn. There are possibly a couple of Vs but it may be a pattern rather than a real inscription.
NARC-1BF3E7		MOUNT	Part of a cast copper alloy figurative mount, probably depicting a saint. The mount would have been attached to a Limoges crucifix, casket or chasse. The preserved fragment comprises a stylised head and the upper part of the torso. The body of the figure is convex and retains traces of decoration that may relate to the

Old Find ID	Image	Object Type	Description
			rendering of clothing. The neck is short and narrow, and the head sub-oval in profile, with a flat top. Facial detail is rudimentary, consisting simply of two small eyes (probably metal pins); any further features are now lost. It is 27.9mm high, 14.7mm at its widest point (at shoulders) and the body is 5.2mm thick and the head is 7.6mm thick. Similar, more complete examples can be seen on the PAS database: LIN 9833AO/ BH-CED505. See also B. Read, *Metal Artefacts of Antiquity* (Portcullis Publishing, 2001), Vol. 1, p. 18 and London Museum, *Medieval Catalogue* (2nd edn, 1967), p. 288.
WAW-EF1B76		SPUR	A cast copper alloy spur. The spur is a distorted asymmetrical? U? shape in plan. The distortion is due to damage and to one terminal being missing. This break was probably quite recent. In profile the arm of the undistorted portion is gently curved, terminating with two integral loops forming A? B? shape. The spur arm and loops for a sidelong? T? shape in plan. The arm is sub-semi-circle in section. At the original apex of the outer edge there is an integral rod which is circular in section with a broken terminal. The spur is undecorated. The surface of the spur has areas of a well-developed mid-green patina. Otherwise, the surface is slightly abraded. It measures 74.99mm long from the terminal arm to the apex, 9.14mm wide and weighs 13.6g. The position of the loops to the arm of the spur suggests a post-medieval date rather than a medieval one.
LEIC-DCFF44		HARNESS PENDANT	Medieval copper alloy and enamel harness pendant, 28mm long, 20mm wide and 4mm thick. The object is in fair condition and weighs 3g. The object is hexagonal with elongated pointed corners. It has a fleur shaped terminal below what would have been the suspension loop. Its surface

Old Find ID	Image	Object Type	Description
			is decorated with a quatrefoil enamel cell with red and blue enamel filling each half. It is filled with a flower like motif formed of a base circle with three lines emerging from it and terminating in a roundel. The object probably would have had a separate scalloped border surrounding it.
LEIC-02DB27		CHAPE	Medieval or post-medieval copper alloy sword chape, 34mm long, 30mm wide, 2mm thick and weighs 12.04g. The object comprises two identical components which has a broadly triangular form with a small pointed projection in the centre of the upper, flat edge. Each one is curved slightly and fits together well. The surface appears to have been tinned or silvered.
LEIC-D0F496		MOUNT	Late medieval/early post-medieval copper alloy and enamel mount, 31mm long, 19mm wide and 3mm thick. The object is oval in form with two rounded protrusions at each end. It is decorated with a foliate motif surrounded by a blue enamel field. Its reverse contains two circular sectioned shafts, one of which still has leather attached.
LEIC-5622A1		SPUR	Medieval? copper alloy spur fragment? It is 28mm long, 14mm wide and 4mm thick. The object has a rectangular section and is sub-rectangular in form. It is incomplete and consists of two circular voids (forming loops) set at either end of a slightly curved plate. At one end there is a clean break at the start of what may be a shaft with a rounded upper surface?
LEIC-BE51B2		STUD	Medieval copper alloy decorative stud, 27mm long, 28mm wide and 3mm thick. The object consists of a rectangular head which is decorated with a man on horseback riding right. It has a large tapering rectangular sectioned tang 17mm long and 8mm wide.

Old Find ID	Image	Object Type	Description
LEIC-849052		MOUNT	Medieval? copper alloy mount, 22mm long, 14mm wide and 5mm thick. The object is in fair condition with a green patina and weighs 4.55g. The object is rectangular in form and section and is decorated with a 'Maltese'-style cross and a possible line of raised triangles along one edge. The reverse has three circular prongs intact which would have secured it. It is probably a belt mount of some sort.
LEIC-F8BC34		COIN	Medieval silver Spanish half real? The coin is very worn.
LEIC-ABCD44		MOUNT	Medieval? copper alloy and gilt mount, 29mm long, 20mm wide, 4mm thick and weighs 6.84g. The object is T-shaped and in two pieces which loosely fit together. It has a greenish-brown patina and the upper portion has traces of heavy gilding. The lower portion has a rounded, splayed terminal with three circular depressions on the upper and lower surfaces which may originally have been holes. The object is unusual as the central part appears to be made of wood on the upper surface with a copper ferrule. It looks as if it has been made to fit around this piece of wood, perhaps it represents a holy relic? The reverse has two robust rivets side by side on the horizontal bar of the T.
LEIC-AD5FB1		SEAL MATRIX	Medieval? Lead-alloy lentoid seal matrix, 34mm long, 25mm wide, 4mm thick and weighs 16.21g. The object has a beige patina and its edge has been chipped away in several places. The matrix is too worn to be clearly seen, but a flower motif and a possible orb-like object can be seen. The lettering is also too faint to read.

Old Find ID	Image	Object Type	Description
			Unusually the reverse is decorated in relief. It has a small semi-circular handle 6mm wide and 3mm high, below this, taking up all the surface, is a lis with the central part in high relief.
LEIC-5BC385		BOOK FITTING	Late medieval copper alloy book fitting, 1350–1500.The object is sub-rectangular in form and cross section and consists of a rectangular shaft which is missing its lower side. This is inscribed with cross-hatched Gothic lettering which is surrounded by a solid border. The lettering probably reads ihc. There is a central rounded rivet, centrally placed, close to the current edge, which is damaged. The complete end has cut-away corners which run into the edges of a raised parallelogram-shaped area. This has some decoration on its surface but is corroded and its base has a central circular hole. On the opposite side of this the object narrows to a sub-triangular projection. This has two concave parallel diagonal depressions on each side, which create a stylised animal's snout. This terminates in an integral suspension loop. The object is heavily gilded all over but is covered with corrosion product. There are the remnants of a shrivelled leather strap on the back. The object has been treated with electrolysis. The object is very similar to SF-1A7DC9 GLO-DDB4D5, IOW-6B705B and NMS-AF7512. It is 50mm long, 15mm wide, 7mm thick and weighs 13.33g.
LEIC-656F02		COIN	Late medieval silver soldino of Venice, 12mm in diameter, 0.5mm thick and weighs 0.29g.

Old Find ID	Image	Object Type	Description
LEIC-34ACA4		CHAPE	Medieval copper alloy dagger scabbard chape, 65mm long, 26mm wide and 3mm thick. The object is in fair condition with a dark-green patina and weighs 8.32g. The object is sub-triangular in form with one straight edge and one long curved edge which meets a diagonally aligned upper edge. The upper edge is decorated with a row of semi-circular protrusions, below which are three circular holes of differing size. Below these is a raised border which runs diagonally along the object. It has rounded edges and its pointed base has a spherical knop terminal.
LEIC-A76A10		HARNESS PENDANT	Medieval copper alloy harness pendant, 43mm long, 31mm wide and 3mm thick. The object is in good condition with a brown/green patina and weighs 11.59g. The object has a rhombus (diamond) form and an integral suspension loop 6mm in diameter. The decoration is very fine and consists of an ornate red lion standing on its hind legs. This is contained in a white border, consisting of a six-petalled flower in each corner which is joined by a row of three solid semi-circles.
LEIC-E34DBC		HARNESS PENDANT	Medieval copper alloy harness pendant, 36mm long, 21mm wide, 1mm thick and weighs 3.77g. The object consists of about half of a circular harness pendent, with a triangular projection forming the base of a suspension loop. The fragment is bent and worn but an incised border *c.* 4mm in from the edge can be seen on one face, which may contain a pattern or an inscription?

Old Find ID	Image	Object Type	Description
LEIC-5E00B6		MOUNT	Copper alloy mount, 28mm in diameter and 6mm high. The mount has a quatrefoil form consisting of four domes which merge together to form a central cross-shaped depression. The mount is hollow and has its rivet attached, its missing one quarter of its edge. It is quite corroded giving it a green and red patina, but it appears to have very slight traces of gilt? Given its form it is probably medieval.
LEIC-757948		MOUNT	Medieval copper alloy belt mount, 15mm long, 13mm wide, 5mm thick and weighs 3.14g. The mount is sub-rectangular in form and D-shaped in cross section. It has a zoomorphic animal head form, with a projecting sub-rectangular snout flanked by eyes and a cross-hatched head with slightly projecting rounded ears at each side. There is a single rivet centrally placed and the underside is hollow. They bear a resemblance to bar mounts with cross-hatched domed centres, of the type found in contexts of *c.* 1350–*c.* 1400 (Peter Egan and Frances Pritchard, *Dress Accessories, c.1150 to c.1450: Medieval Finds from Excavations in London* (Stationery Office Books, 1991), nos 1160–1162) so may also be of this approximate date.
LEIC-82A1FD		SEAL MATRIX	Medieval silver seal matrix. The object has a trilobed terminal which joins a hexagonal section shaft. The shaft widens to contain a circular matrix. This is formed of a central motif with inscription S'ARAZENTE. The motif has a solid circular border which contains a six-pointed, star like border with Gothic trilobed decoration in the spaces formed between the two borders. Inside this is a Crowned Gothic M, probably representing the Virgin Mary. Object recorded from a photograph, so no measurements or weight are currently available.

Old Find ID	Image	Object Type	Description
LEIC-4AFD6B		HARNESS PENDANT	Medieval copper alloy heraldic harness pendant, 34mm in length, 21mm wide, 2mm thick and weighs 4.07g. The object is scutiform with a rectangular cross section. It is in poor condition with incomplete edges and has an incomplete suspension loop emerging from the centre of its straight upper edge. The pendant has a raised area of white enamel in the form of a lion/big cat which is crouching left and has a very long tail.
LEIC-6B072B		DAGGER	Medieval or post-medieval copper alloy dagger quillon (cross-guard), 49mm long, 29mm wide, 6mm thick and weighs 26.51g. The object consists of a rectangular cross-sectioned shaft with slightly flared rounded edges. The shaft widens in its centre, forming two triangular projections which flank a rectangular hole which would have accommodated the dagger tang. To one side of this there is a double-looped projection, forming a W shape with a rectangular cross section, the ends of which emerge from between the central projection and the terminal, and would have acted as a guard. This is unusual as most have a triangular projection here, see PAS database https://finds.org.uk/: HAMP-C87776, but we do have one parallel for this unusual shape, NLM-A04FA3, which has been dated to the post-medieval period.
LEIC-3E99F6		COIN	Medieval silver Venetian soldino of Doge Michael Steno, 1400–13.

Old Find ID	Image	Object Type	Description
LEIC-00ADA2		HARNESS PENDANT	Medieval copper alloy and enamel horse harness pendant, 31mm long, 22mm wide, 2mm thick and weighs 4.92g. The object is in poor condition, missing its edges and some surface, and has a brown patina. The object is now sub-triangular in form and has the remains of a suspension loop in its upper surface. Its surface is largely covered in blue enamel which has recesses where other material has been. The pattern appears to be a series of diagonal lines separating animal motifs, possibly lions, the Bohun arms.
LEIC-573F32		HARNESS HOOK	Medieval copper alloy harness mount, 50mm long, 22mm wide, 9mm thick at hook and weighs 13.64g. The object is in fair condition. The object consists of a triangular plate which is decorated on both surfaces with slightly embossed, foliate decoration. The lower pointed edge holds a raised rectangular collar which sits above a circular sectioned hook. There are no obvious breaks, but also no fixing holes. The object may relate to harness mounts identified by Nick Griffiths. His Finds Research Group datasheet, www.findsresearchgroup.com › datasheets-vol-i, on shield-shaped mounts discusses these. He says: 'Finally and of uncertain purpose is a small group of shields, double sided (some repeat the same design, others have different designs) at the top of a rod or bar curved into a hook'.
LEIC-F51C3D		STAMP	Late medieval to early post-medieval copper alloy stamp (1350–1650), 41mm long, 15mm diameter and weighs 23.9g. The object consists of a rectangular cross-sectioned tapering shaft, 6 x 7mm wide, which sits below a rectangular shaped and cross-sectioned 'head', 10 x 10mm wide, which terminates in a rectangular cross-sectioned, circular

Old Find ID	Image	Object Type	Description
			shaped die. The die is engraved with a muscular horned bull with his tail upright. Kevin Leahy, PAS National Finds Adviser, has identified this as a leather worker's stamp.
WAW-FB178C		MOUNT	Medieval (thirteenth–fifteenth century) mount. It is shield-shaped and on the outer face has a low-relief frame. The mount is possibly decorated, but if so corrosion has distorted the design and it is not visible. There are slight domes, one towards the upper edge and the other towards the lower edge, which may be a rivet head, although the rivet is not visible on the reverse. The reverse is undecorated. The mount has a grey patina and measures 28.02mm long, 19.21mm wide, 2.61mm thick and weighs 4.79g.
LEIC-60CFFD		HARNESS PENDANT	Medieval copper alloy harness pendant, 30mm long, 21mm wide, 2mm thick and weighs 4.29g. The object is sub-circular in form and rectangular in cross section. It has four rounded edges joined by slight triangular projections which correspond to the corners of a rectangular motif in the centre of the object. This has a solid, slightly raised border and appears to contain a lion passant. The outer side of this border may have slight projections which are surrounded by a field of red enamel, though the object's surface is so worn it is difficult to be certain. The triangular projections may also have held enamel or similar and appear to contain circular borders? The reverse is plain, and the object has an integral transverse suspension loop.

Old Find ID	Image	Object Type	Description
LEIC-C58FA6		MOUNT	Late medieval? copper alloy mount, 20mm long and 12mm wide. The mount is lozenge-shaped and its surface is decorated with a stylised flower consisting of a central circle surrounded by four lozenge-shaped petals, which fit into each corner of the mount and are contained by a narrow border. The reverse has the remains of a rectangular shaft which is set slightly off centre.
LEIC-A28B17		COIN	Gold quarter noble of Edward III, 1351–77, London.
LEIC-5835F5		SEAL MATRIX	Medieval copper alloy seal matrix of Roger of Trafford, 34mm long, 31mm wide, 7mm thick and weighs 7.04g. The object is in good condition. The matrix is lentoid in form and has an integral circular suspension loop/handle on its reverse upper edge. It is decorated with an image of one bird of prey swooping on another. Above this is a left-facing (anti-clockwise) swastika. The inscription reads 'S'ROGERI OE TRAFFORD+'.
LEIC-70B476		RING	Medieval copper alloy finger ring, 26mm long, 11mm wide, 3mm thick and weighs 4.37g. The ring is incomplete, missing part of its hoop which has an oval cross section and is plain. This widens out to accommodate an oval bezel, marked by an incised border. This contains a capital 'I' with an incised crown motif above it, formed of an incised horizontal line with four diagonal ones emanating from it. Signet rings with a crowned initial and branches to each side became increasingly common in the fifteenth century, and it is thought the initial was for the owner's first name and I (for J) is popular (P.D.A. Harvey and Andrew

Old Find ID	Image	Object Type	Description
			McGuinness, *A Guide to British Medieval Seals* (Toronto University Press, 1996), p. 93). Many similar rings can be seen on this database, e.g. BH-CA395D SUSS-D1CD32, LON-2B8E94 and SOM-29C9A7.
LEIC-8C1487		CHAPE	Medieval? copper alloy sword chape, 36mm long and 21mm wide. The chape has a greenish/grey patina and has snapped off along its upper edge. It has a rounded base and straight sides and is decorated with a series of raised vertical lines. The object is 5mm thick and appears to have been cast.
NARC-2F52B7		SEAL MATRIX	Cast copper alloy seal matrix, medieval, probably fifteenth century. Circular seal tapering upwards to a cone hexagonal in section. A suspension loop is attached to the end of the cone after a small collar. The hole in the suspension loop is 2mm in diameter. The seal is 17mm in diameter and 30mm high. The collar is 7mm in diameter and the suspension loop area is 10mm deep. The seal on the base is a coat of arms. Straight-topped shield. The seal is very corroded. It appears to be split into three sections separated with a groove with a circular motif close to each corner.
LEIC-117843		CHAPE	Medieval or post-medieval copper alloy chape, 24mm long, 6mm in diameter at its open end and weighs 2.05g. The object consists of a sheet of copper alloy that has been folded to form a cone with a very elongated point. The object could be a strap or lace chape.

Old Find ID	Image	Object Type	Description
WAW-916B45		MOUNT	Medieval (thirteenth to fourteenth century) quatrefoil-shaped mount. The copper alloy fitting has a quatrefoil-shaped plaque which has an integral stud protruding from the centre of the reverse. The stud is square sectioned and tapers to a flat terminal. The mount is decorated on the outer face with a central capital I with a possible martlet above and an identifiable motif either side. There are no traces of enamel which is often found on such mounts. The surface of the mount is heavily abraded, but has traces of a mid- to dark-green patina, otherwise it has a dark-brown-coloured surface. The object is 40.15mm long, 39.98mm wide, 9.86mm thick and weighs 15.72g. The stud/mount possibly decorated a harness and is likely to date to the thirteenth to fourteenth centuries, based on the style and surface decoration.
LEIC-B3B238		SEAL MATRIX	Medieval lead alloy seal matrix, 32mm long, 20mm wide, 4mm thick and weighs 14.54g. The object is in fair condition with a grey patina. The object is oval in form and rectangular in section. It has a small circular 'handle' at the upper edge of its reverse which sits above a rectangular sectioned rib. The surface of the matrix is plain, perhaps it was being prepared to be re-used?
LEIC-172A61		SEAL MATRIX	Medieval copper alloy pendant seal, 21mm in diameter. The central motif appears to show a warhorse and rider. The legend is not legible and the edges are too fragile to take an impression. From the illustration, this object appears to be a seal matrix with a hexagonally faceted handle rising to a rounded pierced terminal. The circular die appears to show a lamb and flag (Agnus Dei) design as the central motif, with the lamb in profile facing left with the flagpole

Old Find ID	Image	Object Type	Description
			passing behind the body. The inscription could well be * ECCE AGNUS DEI, the most common inscription on matrices with this central design. Fourteenth century.
NARC-5D1753		PILGRIM BADGE	A copper-alloy mount in the shape of a scallop shell, quite possibly a pilgrim badge of medieval date. The scallop shell was associated with the pilgrimage site of St James of Santiago de Compostela in Spain, which became one of the most important pilgrimage centres in medieval Europe (Brian Spencer, *Pilgrim Souvenirs and Secular Badges* (Museum of London, 1998), p. 244). The scallop shell then became a ubiquitous symbol for pilgrimage more generally. This example is slightly rounded on the front and dished on the reverse. There are two broken attachment lugs on the reverse. It measures 22.85mm long, 22.1mm wide, 2.84mm thick and weighs 3.3g. Similar, slightly more elaborately decorated examples in a range of metals are recorded by Spencer (1998, p. 246, figs 249–50). Spencer notes how it can be difficult to determine whether all examples were truly pilgrim souvenirs, and some may simply have been locally made decorative mounts, worn by devotees of St James (Spencer, 1998, p. 247).
LEIC-F0AC04		HARNESS PENDANT	Medieval copper alloy harness pendant, 34mm long, 33mm wide, 6mm thick and weighs 15.35g. The object is in fair condition but has been folded. It appears to consist of two rectangular plates which are joined by a hinge mechanism. There is also another section protruding to one side which may be part of a fixing plate. Each of the rectangular plates is decorated with a motif resembling a scallop shell and consisting of sub-rectangular cells filled with white enamel. This sits in a shield (cabochon) shaped border infilled with red enamel.

Old Find ID	Image	Object Type	Description
LEIC-4814F7		MOUNT	Medieval copper alloy dog-headed mount, 33mm long, 15mm wide and weighs 12.92g. The object consists of a 3D dog's head which has a barrel-shaped snout with projecting tongue, a slightly wider head with incisions representing eyes and triangular ears emerging from the top. Behind it has a sub-rectangular shaped and cross-sectioned neck which flattens and then divides, projecting at a diagonal. At this point it has snapped but appears to be forming an inner circular/semi-circular void with a frame around?
LEIC-A6C834		BADGE	Late medieval silver badge in the form of a male boar, complete except for the lower part of three of its four legs. The boar is seen in profile, facing left. It has an open mouth, long nose and prominent tusks; the ears are pointed and the left ear, closer to the viewer, has a recessed centre. A row of upright, slightly rearward-pointing bristles runs all the way along the back from the thick neck to the curled-up tail. Much of both right legs are missing, but more survives of the front left leg and the rear left leg is still complete. Under the tail is a prominent testicle, and between and in front of the rear legs is a forward-pointing penis. There are patches of gilding behind its ears, on the tail and across the row of bristles along its back. This would suggest that the whole surface was originally thickly gilded. The reverse contains a single sub-rectangular patch of solder, which would have held a pin in place. It measures 28mm long, 15mm high and 2mm thick. The object weighs 3.25g and is in fair condition. It dates to the late fifteenth century. The boar was the livery badge of the household of Richard III. The badge was found during the search for the Battle

Old Find ID	Image	Object Type	Description
			of Bosworth field and provides good evidence for the presence of a member of the king's personal household in the area. It thus adds weight to the other archaeological evidence, which has now located the battlefield and thus the site of Richard III's death.
LEIC-4405A7		BADGE	Late medieval (late fifteenth-century) silver gilt dress fitting, 'cap badge', 15mm wide and 14mm high. This dress fitting is in the form of an eagle with outstretched wings, its head bent towards its left wing. The bird stands on a branch and has a snake in its mouth. On the reverse is a centrally placed circular sectioned rod, the function of which is unclear. The dress fitting resembles pilgrim badges from the late medieval period and is similar in technique to a number of Tudor belt mounts and dress fittings. This object was found as part of the Bosworth battlefield survey. Kevin Schurer Emeritus Professor of English Local History, Leicester University, has recently (2017) identified this item as probably being a fettered falcon; the head is facing to the right, a sign of illegitimacy. It could therefore be the livery badge of Arthur Plantagenet, illegitimate son of King Edward IV. There is no record of Arthur being present at Bosworth, but he was of fighting age, being born between 1461 and 1475. We know he survived and served in the court of his half-sister, Elizabeth of York, and became an Esquire of the King's Bodyguard to his nephew Henry VIII, to whom he was a close companion. He died of a heart attack in 1540, two days after being released from the Tower, after being held (incorrectly) on suspicion of treason over Calais, where he was born and had been Constable.

Old Find ID	Image	Object Type	Description
LEIC-88E3F1		FINGER RING	Medieval gold finger ring, 19mm in diameter and weighs 1.26g. The ring has a rectangular box-like bezel which is 6mm long and wide and 2mm high. It has an oval recess in its upper surface and contains a red oval stone, possibly a garnet, which has become detached and is now stuck at an angle inside the bezel. It has a plain rectangular sectioned band, which has small rectangular shoulders with linear incisions running across it. These sit either side of an integral rectangular plate which holds the bezel. The object dates from the twelfth or thirteenth century and has close parallels, particularly 2004 T133, 2004T 495 and 2006 T63, PAS Database, https://finds.org.uk/.
LEIC-E84347		INKWELL	Medieval or post-medieval lead-alloy object, 58mm wide, 48mm thick, 43mm high and weighs 318g. The object is in fair condition. It is sub-triangular in section and form with a small circular hole in its upper surface. Both this and the base have a protruding rounded lip. It is decorated with a series of incised vertical lines which separate rounded, bulging sections. The object is believed to be an inkwell.
LEIC-69C282		MOUNT	Medieval or post-medieval copper alloy mount, 40mm long, 22mm wide, 4mm thick and weighs 9.65g. The object is in fair condition with a dark brown patina. The object has a rounded upper section which terminates in a rounded protrusion. Below this the object is lozenge-shaped and narrows slightly which gives the impression it is forming a shaft? The object has two semi-circular depressions at the top and faint traces of a raised area inside the lozenge. The object is slightly hollow on the reverse which indicates it is only to be seen from the front. It

Old Find ID	Image	Object Type	Description
			may be a strap mount, or it could be part of a looped mount, which were designed for carrying keys.
WMID-9E0EE8		COIN	A complete, medieval, silver groat of James II of Scotland (1437–60), Second Coinage issue, dating to the period 1451–60. Initial mark: cross pattee. Reverse initial mark: sun or starburst before V in inner legend. Mint of Edinburgh. Spink (2003), p. 34, No. 5231. It is 26.3mm in diameter, 1.1mm thick and weighs 3.7g. The Spink catalogue is published yearly, and is the standard catalogue for the coins of England. The prices listed for common coins reflect average prices that a dealer will charge for a coin, but not what they will pay for a coin. The prices shown for rarer coins usually reflect the most recent auction prices for coins, and are fairly reliable.
WMID-94D461		SEAL MATRIX	An incomplete medieval (1250–1400) cast-copper alloy pedestal/pendant seal matrix. The body of the matrix consists of a pedestal formed from six irregular tapering sides. These terminate in a single moulded band, comprising three horizontal ribs, below a probable sub-triangular pointed loop. The suspension loop is incomplete. No orientation marks are present around the base of the matrix. The die or seal face is broadly circular in plan, with a diameter of 18.64mm. The die/seal face is incomplete, with the edges being damaged. The die is well cut and detailed. The central device of the seal depicts a standing female figure, holding a small child, facing an individual with hands held up in prayer. The female figure is meant to depict the Virgin Mary, holding the infant Jesus. None of the lettering around the outside of the matrix remains legible. The matrix is 19.53mm high and the base diameter

Old Find ID	Image	Object Type	Description
			is 18.64 mm. The top of the pedestal is 5.95mm thick. It weighs 8g. The matrix is a mid- to dark-brown colour, with an even surface patina covering the majority of the surface.
LEIC-C51C57		CANNON BALL	Two metal (either lead or copper alloy?) cannon shot, both are 39mm in diameter and each weighs 340g. Found together in a garden.
LEIC-66CD92		FINGER RING	A gold fifteenth-century posy ring, 18mm in diameter. The surface is decorated with an unbroken groove running along the upper and lower edge with floral sprays engraved into its surface in between. Punctuating the decoration are three black-letter words. One is easy to read, 'a', another may be 'ma', the third appears to be 'vie' which would read 'a ma vie' (to my heart).
LEIC-5A2397		MOUNT	Medieval copper alloy belt mount, 26mm long, 9mm wide, 14mm deep and weighs 2.71g. The object is in fair condition with a reddish patina. The object is quite worn and is rectangular in form. It has two semi-circular sectioned shafts, which have been bent over, protruding from its base. The surface is decorated with a trefoil terminal at each end and a central oval section which appears to have foliate decoration.
WAW-176004		HARNESS PENDANT	Cast copper alloy horse-harness pendant, possibly. It has a circular body with eight integral trifoliate knops on a short stem. Only two of the knops are complete. The body of the pendant has a high-relief four-legged animal passant, possibly a lion. In the field around the animal there is a series of glossy, shiny hard red enamel patches. The enamel sits on the surface of the object and is not

Old Find ID	Image	Object Type	Description
			set with a low-relief cell. Around the edge of the pendant's body there is no lip remaining. The reverse of the pendant is undecorated. The surface of the mount is heavily abraded and corroded with large areas having a rough red/brown colour and there are traces of green, but this is not a developed patina. The pendant is 29.49mm long, 32.95mm wide and weighs 7.8g. The artefact is possibly a harness pendant but the upper most knop, though incomplete, is not the usual integral loop which you find on medieval harness pendants. The condition of the enamel also looks unusual, but equally could be medieval, and has undergone a particularly heated treatment. If this is a harness pendant it probably dates to the medieval period and they were most popular in the thirteenth and early fourteenth centuries (N. Griffiths, 'Horse Harness Pendants', Finds Research Group Datasheet No. 5' (1986)).
LEIC-056933		SEAL MATRIX	Medieval copper alloy seal matrix, 16mm in diameter, 11mm high and weighs 4.02g. The object has a dark-green patina with some surface pitting. The object has a hexagonal tapering shaft which has broken off. The seal depicts a kneeling lamb (Agnes Dei) which has a cross on a shaft above it. Halfway down the shaft is a triangular flag of St George. The border contains an inscription of possibly seven letters, which Malcolm Jones, from the University of Sheffield, believes reads PRIVE SV.

Old Find ID	Image	Object Type	Description
LEIC-95A972		SEAL MATRIX	Medieval copper alloy seal matrix, 18mm long and 14mm in diameter. The seal has a tapering hexagonal shaft 14mm long which has an integral, indented loop terminal 4mm long. The matrix is circular but has some damage to its edges. It is very worn, and no inscription can be made out, but the centre seems to show a bird of some sort.
LEIC-5C37C0		SEAL MATRIX	Medieval lead-alloy seal matrix fragment, 94mm long, 27mm wide and it weighs 75g. The object is in fair condition with a beige patina. It has been twisted and fractured. The object is about half of an oval or lentoid shaped matrix and has an inscribed border. The object is illustrated with part of a human figure, the arm and edge of the body can be seen. The arm is holding a staff similar to a bishop's crozier, and a triangular purse? is suspended from its wrist. The inscription reads S[…] TVMERNOLD. Malcolm Jones, University of Sheffield, has suggested this should read S[ECRE]TVM ERNOLD[I], 'seal of Ernold'.
LEIC-02E2F1		CHAPE	Medieval copper alloy sword chape, 17mm high, 21mm wide, 6mm thick and weighs 4.5g. The object is in fair condition with a green patina. The chape is trapezoidal in form with the narrower end, 15mm wide, making up the base. It is made from one piece which has been folded over to form the two sides. The front is decorated with radiating incised lines and has a shaped upper edge, with a rounded knop at each end of a horizontal edge which has a small circular cut-out in the centre. The reverse echoes the same form but it is missing about half of its area, this is also plain.

Old Find ID	Image	Object Type	Description
LEIC-6499C2		HARNESS PENDANT	Medieval copper alloy and enamel horse harness pendant, 45mm long, 27mm wide and and weighs 8.09g. The object is in a fair condition. It is shield-shaped and has a suspension loop centrally placed on its upper edge. It is decorated with five left-facing 'rook-like' birds which are surrounded by red enamel. The birds are divided into two rows, three at the top and two at the bottom, by a broad raised horizontal band.
LEIC-0B5D67		MOUNT	Medieval copper alloy complete stud mount, 31mm in diameter and 2mm thick. It is circular and decorated with tiny punched triangles arranged as a cross within an oval within a wavy edged circle within a plain-edged circle. The spike at the back is central and has a square section.
LEIC-10AC8D		FINGER RING	Medieval gold finger ring, 27mm long, 7mm wide, 1mm thick and weighs 3.71g. The ring has a rectangular cross section and has been flattened and has a clean cut-through the loop. The decoration on each cut edge would join up, so there is no portion of the object missing. One edge is bent slightly upwards and corresponds to some crumpling damage at the point where it is bent over itself. The other portion sits neatly over the loop and has a 'clean' bend. The ring is decorated with a plain raised border at each edge and inside this is a series of five diagonally placed dotted lines which separate four rhomboid raised frames. These contain a central circular flower flanked by two triangular foliate motifs. The inner part of the loop is engraved with a single three? letter word in a square Gothic script. The lettering and decoration suggests a late medieval date, probably fifteenth century, for the object.

Old Find ID	Image	Object Type	Description
LEIC-D903CC		HARNESS PENDANT	Medieval copper alloy harness pendant, 36mm long, 24mm wide, 4mm thick and weighs 8.43g. The object is scutiform (shield-shaped) with a straight top and sides curving to a point. There is an incomplete suspension loop in the centre of its upper edge. The design, now damaged, consists of two fields of blue enamel with a diagonal band in its centre, running from top left to bottom right (a bend cotised). The upper right panel has a small patch of gilding, suggesting a now damaged motif here. Rob Webley, from Exeter University, has suggested these are the arms of the Bohun family, which are a bend cotised between six lioncels rampant. There are many parallels on the PAS database: ESS-2313DE is particularly well preserved.
LEIC-349582		FINGER RING	Medieval copper alloy finger ring 19mm long, 13mm wide and weighs 3.99g. The ring is in a fair condition with a red/brown patina. The object consists of the bezel and shoulders, the rest has snapped off in antiquity. The bezel is oval in form and 2mm thick. It shows a long-necked bird, probably a swan, standing facing left with its wings outspread. The engraving is enclosed by an incised border very close to its edge and the shoulders, which are the width of the oval, emerge from its lower edge. The shoulders taper sharply in thickness and width to become a quite delicate rounded shaft, 2mm wide, with no obvious signs of decoration.
IHS-891316		HARNESS PENDANT	A copper alloy shield-shaped harness pendant, suspension loop intact. Red enamel remains on two bars and three pellets above; the original arms will have been? 'or' (gold), two bars 'gules' (red) and in 'chief three torteaux' (3 red circles). It measures 25 x 40 mm.

Old Find ID	Image	Object Type	Description
IHS-AB8EE7	† SIGILL' IOH B OAIS	SEAL MATRIX	A lead circular seal matrix, back with cast design of inverted iris flower, suspension loop apparently intact at top of same but with no sign of a perforation. The projection may simply be intended for use as a grip when sealing. Device of a neat six-petalled flower with raised round centre, separated from the lettering by a fine line (forming an uneven circle), with a similar line marking the outer edge of the matrix. Inscription reads +S'IGILL' IOH':BOV AIS (Latin: The Seal of John Bovais). There is a cut across the matrix through the 'O' and 'V' and also affecting one of the octofoil's petals, and this damage must have occurred after the matrix was engraved. The surname BOVAIS may be a contraction of the medieval Latin *bovarius*, meaning 'a herdsman', but this sense is not found in P.H. Reaney and R.M. Wilson's *A Dictionary of British Surnames* (Routledge & Kegan Paul, 1976). Instead, there are several variants listed under Beaves which indicate an origin in the French place name Beauvais in the Oise region of France. It is likely, therefore, that this seal belonged to John Beauvais; the corresponding modern name would probably be something like John Bovis. It measures 23mm in diameter and weighs 11g.
LEIC-F85D01		COIN	Medieval silver gros tournois of Phillip IV of France, 1295–1314.

Old Find ID	Image	Object Type	Description
LEIC-93C145		SEAL MATRIX	Medieval copper alloy seal matrix, 21mm in diameter, 2mm thick and weighs 4.37g. The object is circular in form and rectangular in cross section. The matrix is decorated with the 'lamb of god' carrying a banner in the centre with an inscription contained in the border which reads ECCE AGNVS DEI – behold the lamb of god. See PAS database: KENT-B00194.
LEIC-93D304		SEAL MATRIX	Medieval copper alloy seal matrix, 21mm in diameter, 2mm thick and weighs 4.37g. The object consists of a short hexagonal tapering shaft with a double collar sitting below a large integral suspension loop, which is filled with iron corrosion. The shaft terminates in a shield-shaped matrix, 13 x 14mm. This depicts Mary suckling Jesus, its edges are worn so the inscription is hard to read, possibly reads RO––EDIV.
LEIC-935918		WEIGHT	Medieval lead-alloy shield-shaped weight, 28mm long, 25mm wide, 9mm thick and weighs 29.58g. The object is sub-triangular in form and rectangular in cross section. It has a scutiform shape with a lower lipped edge. It is decorated on its upper surface with a possible lion passant, a curved tail and part of a body are just visible.
LEIC-946183		STRAP FITTING	Medieval shield-shaped strap fitting or mount, copper alloy, 37mm long and 14mm at widest point. The object is an elongated triangular shaped shield with a small circle at its base. It has upward pointing top corners on either side of a trefoil motif. Its surface shows traces of gilding, but it is corroded, and no surface pattern can be seen. On its reverse it has a rivet behind the trefoil motif which points upwards. Near the base is a second rivet, this one has snapped off, but there is a fine

Old Find ID	Image	Object Type	Description
			piece of cloth (linen?) still attached to the mount. The back also shows a fracture line, which can just be made out on the upper surface, this appears to have been repaired.
LEIC-96C553	2007 T227	FINGER RING	A fragment from a medieval finger ring, which would have formed the bezel. The motif is a heart sprouting flowers below a foliated crown. On the reverse can be seen the remains of the flat band of the hoop. Fragment is silver gilt and dates from the late fifteenth or early sixteenth centuries.
LEIC-96E623		CRUCIFIX	Late medieval silver gilt crucifix, 21mm long, 10mm wide, 3mm thick and weighs 2.53g. The object is rectangular in form and cross section and depicts Jesus on the cross, with a large halo behind his head and curved outstretched arms with over large hands fixed to a narrow cross beam. He is flanked by two shorter figures whose heads reach the underside of his arms. To the left is the figure of Mary and to the right a male figure, probably St John. Above the figure of Jesus is a wide, short shaft with a large scroll attached that should read INRI but is poorly executed and resembles IRM. The object terminates with a suspension loop of sub-rectangular form with a circular hole, 5 x 4 x 1mm. The object is made of silver and is heavily gilded but is worn off at the corners.
LEIC-2AC5D4		SEAL MATRIX	Medieval copper alloy seal matrix, 33mm long, 21mm wide, 4mm thick and weighs 8.48g. The matrix is ovate in form and rectangular in cross section. It has a small semi-circular loop, 8mm long, with circular hole on the edge of its reverse. The surface has a motif in good condition showing a bird (pelican?) feeding

Old Find ID	Image	Object Type	Description
			three chicks in a nest on a pole, which has fleur like projections at each side. Outside this in a solid border is an inscription that reads KI BEN: EYME: TART:OBLIE, which is a medieval French proverb – 'Qui bien aime, a tart oublié', meaning 'He who loves well takes a long time to forget'. Thanks to Kris Didden for the translation.
LEIC-B9E481		SEAL MATRIX	Late medieval lead-alloy seal matrix, 79mm long, 47mm wide, 6mm thick and weighs 136g. The seal has a pointed oval form and a rectangular cross section. It has a flat reverse with no loop but a small depressed area that may have held one. The matrix has a rather crude image of a bishop? with the head squashed into the point and very square body with feet protruding from the hem of his garment. The figure is holding a cross-headed shaft, with left hand raised in benediction. His garment is decorated with a double-chevron border running from its shoulders with the point on the chest and four small vertical lines running from this up to the top of the shoulder. The hem has a rope-like border contained in a solid upper line. The inscription reads +SIGILhEN [retrograde] RIC .ARChIE [retrograde] PISCOPI OR [retrograde] DWE [retrograde] LI N [retrograde] O, which translates as 'Seal of Henry, Archbishop of Orwell'. The seal is of a very inferior material for an official ecclesiastical seal and given the place name cannot be an attempt at a forgery. Malcolm Jones of Sheffield University has suggested it is perhaps akin to boy bishop tokens? The tokens are connected with a late medieval tradition celebrating St Nicholas, in which a boy would be elected 'bishop' on December feast days and give a sermon. The tokens are found

Old Find ID	Image	Object Type	Description
			largely in East Anglia and there are also records of the boys being given vestments etc. to wear so the granting of a seal may have been part of the festivities.
LEIC-2A9D30		STRAP END	Medieval copper alloy strap end fragment, 30mm long, 23mm wide, 3mm thick and weighs 5.84g. The object consists of a fragment of the lower part of a 'lyre'-shaped strap end. The upper portion is sub-rectangular in form but represents the lower portion of a crescent-shaped fragment. It has two circular rivets present, sitting side by side, below a fragment of a complete edge, with a raised solid border, and sitting above a curved raised line forming the lower edge of the crescent. The upper part has an area of cross-hatched and raised decoration. Below the lower curved line is a 'trefoil'-shaped projection with a series of linear depressions radiating outwards to its edges. The whole surface has traces of gilding. The reverse, which is plain, has traces of silvering all over it. For a complete example please see PAS database: LEIC-29578A HAMP-B9087F and CORN-BD8107.
LEIC-429555		FINGER RING	Medieval silver gilt finger ring fragment (two pieces), 20mm long, 7.5 mm wide, 1.5mm thick (at bezel) and weighs 2.56g. It has a sub-triangular section at the bezel, having a ridge running along it lengthways which gradually flattens into the loop. The ring may have two figures engraved, one on each side of the ridge, but it is unclear. The loop has a repeat diagonal stripe of raised silver dots on a gilded field.

Old Find ID	Image	Object Type	Description
PUBLIC-F044BA		FINGER RING	A cast-copper alloy seal matrix, probably the detached bezel from a signet ring. The object is a flat disc with slightly curved sides, 15.2mm in diameter and 2.3mm thick. The front face has an incised retrograde letter S centrally located which is surrounded by a border of seven irregularly spaced indentations, and there are short incised vertical lines to either side of the S, and a crude arrow shape formed of three lines (possibly an attempt at a palm) between one of them and the outer edge. The rear has a broad mark running transversely across, presumably left by the solder where the hoop was formerly attached.
LEIC-671DB0		COIN	Late medieval silver half real of Ferdinand and Isabella of Spain (1469–1504), dating from 1474–1504.
LEIC-AC0440		HARNESS MOUNT	Medieval copper alloy and gilt pendant suspension mount, 34mm wide, 27mm high and weighs 6.99g. The object consists of a rectangular plate with a protrusion in the centre of its lower edge. The protrusion is formed from a rectangular piece of metal, 8 x 10mm, with a slit in its centre which has been folded over to form two loops. The object is decorated with the recessed image of a bird facing left, which would have originally contained coloured enamel. It can be described as 'Or a bird close azure beaked and legged gules'. The background is decorated with incised cross hatching which has been gilded. There is a rivet hole in each corner of the object which would have been used to attach it to a leather harness strap and the lower loops would have held a dangling pendant. This suspension mount is noted as part of

Old Find ID	Image	Object Type	Description
			a group of similar pendants and hangers by Baker (J. Baker, *The Coat of Arms – The Earliest Armorial Harness Pendants* (The Heraldry Society, 2015), p. 21, n. 78).
LEIC-92A149		PENDANT	Medieval copper alloy harness pendant, 29mm long, 15mm wide, 6mm thick and weighs 3.3g. The object is circular in form and rectangular in cross section and consists of a circular pendant with five small rectangular projections, the sixth one forms a suspension loop for an articulated sub-rectangular belt fitting. This has a partial transverse loop attached to its upper edge and is plain. The pendant is decorated with wheel-like spokes emerging from a central circular boss. Each alternate triangular cell is decorated with red enamel, with possibly dark blue? in the others. The object has traces of tinning/silvering all over its surface.
LEIC-A0F9CC		BOOK FITTING	Medieval copper alloy object, 23mm long, 22mm wide, *c.* 3mm thick and weighs 5.2g. The object has damage to its edges, but its surviving form is circular with a rectangular projection at one end, and generally rectangular in cross section. The projection sticks out to either side, has a flat surface and is decorated with two rows of stamped rectangular depressions. The circular element has a slightly rounded upper edge which creates a V-shaped depression at each side where it joins the rectangular area. The circular part has two circular holes, one centrally placed and one directly above this. This is decorated with a solid slightly raised circular border which is flanked by a row of rectangular depressions on each side. Inside this are four crescents formed of two rows of the rectangular depressions which butt up to the

Old Find ID	Image	Object Type	Description
			border, forming a cruciform-like central void. The decoration is of the type known as interrupted rocker-arm, or rouletting.
LEIC-387565		HARNESS PENDANT	Medieval copper alloy harness pendant, 36mm long, 20mm wide and 3mm thick. The object is in a poor condition with a brown patina and weighs 5.42g. The object is shield-shaped and has lost most of its original surface but may have a slight trace of gilding intact. It has a suspension loop which is circular at its top, but tapers to a point where it joins the main body. This has a circular hole, 2mm in diameter, in its centre.
BUC-C4F713		SEAL MATRIX	A copper alloy pointed oval-shaped seal matrix with an angular suspension loop with a low ridge across the back. The seal face is in poor condition and unreadable.
WMID-7ACA03		KNIFE	Angled copper alloy horse-hoof terminal, probably from a scale tang knife, late fifteenth/early sixteenth century, 20.2mm long, 16.1mm wide, 10.2mm deep and weighs 10.8g. There is a notch in the end and two parallel ridges running around the terminal. On the longer (convex) edge of the terminal there is also a moulded face. There are the remains of the iron tang in a slot in the base. Brown patina, but where this has been lost the terminal has a pitted, light-green powdery surface.

Old Find ID	Image	Object Type	Description
LEIC-31F5E2		HARNESS PENDANT	Medieval copper alloy and gold harness pendant, 27mm long, 21mm wide and 3mm thick. The object is in poor condition with a reddish/brown patina and weighs 5.46g. The pendant is circular in form and has a worn circular? sectioned suspension fitting. The pendant shows a relief image of a lion with a stylised circular mane which is picked out in gold. This is surrounded by a decorative border also picked out in gold.
LEIC-84A867		SEAL MATRIX	Medieval copper alloy pendant seal matrix, 28mm long, 15mm in diameter and 2mm thick. The seal surface shows a bird looking downwards with outstretched wings. The pendant itself is 'clover' shaped and has one large hole in its upper portion with three smaller holes in a horizontal line beneath it. The object is in good condition with a brown patina, although it has some concretions on the shaft and on the seal surface.
NARC-2FCDE5		SPUR	A cast-copper alloy object, probably the rowel from a medieval or early post-medieval spur. It is circular and flattish, and made up of forty-five radiating ridges with grooves between them, all cast together in the centre but becoming separate at the ends. There are deeper separations between each group of five or six straight rods, dividing the circle into eight wedge-shaped parts. Each rod is approximately 25mm long and 1mm in diameter, combining to create a circle *c.* 56mm across. The rods are bent at the end, probably through use. In the centre is a hole, originally circular, now worn to a drop shape. Possibly a wheel from a pastry jigger, but it would only have produced a row of dots on the dough, so much more likely to be a detached spur rowel.

Old Find ID	Image	Object Type	Description
LEIC-4EB498		COIN	Indian or Asian coin, possibly medieval.
LEIC-C38AA8		COIN	Medieval gold ryal of Edward IV, Bristol, Light Coinage, 1464–70.
LEIC-57FC44		COIN	An incomplete medieval gold quarter noble, probably of Richard II (1377–99) with (likely) pellet in centre of reverse. Mint: London. The coin is in poor condition, with approximately a third missing (from the top of the obverse) and a further tear from the missing area across the centre of the coin. The coin is also slightly bent. These appear to be post-depositional effects. It is possible that the coin belongs to the reign of Edward III (1327–77), Treaty Series (1363–9) from the mint at Calais.
LEIC-119010		KNIFE	Medieval copper alloy knife fitting, 20mm long, 10mm wide, 9mm thick and weighs 5.51g. The object has a rectangular form and cross section and is undecorated. One edge has an oval centrally placed hole, which coincides with a larger hole on the opposite edge, which sits within a recess that runs the width of the object. The object would have sat between a knife blade and a handle. The object is very similar to LEIC-933794, see PAS database.

Courtesy of the British Museum's Portable Antiquities Scheme.

A List from the Bosworth Finds Classed as True Battle Finds

A list of 143 finds extracted from the Bosworth Finds Database for recorded finds that are listed as True Battle Finds, as of January 2021.

Find No.	Field No.	Primary Material	Sub Material	Primary Type	Sub Type
124	80	Ag?	Au	Badge	Military?
175	178	Cu alloy	Au	Spur?	
179	185	Cu alloy		Harness pendant	
234	67	Cu alloy		Buckle	
249	24	Cu alloy	Au	Harness pendant	
253	174	Cu alloy		Buckle	
257	187	Cu alloy		Buckle	
263	181	Cu alloy		Strap end	
264	181	Cu alloy		Strap end	
265	181	Cu alloy		Strap end	
267	181	Cu alloy		Strap fitting	
271	181	Cu alloy		Buckle	Spectacle
274	181	Cu alloy		Buckle	
277	181	Cu alloy		Buckle	
279	181	Cu alloy		Buckle	Spur
281	181	Cu alloy		Harness pendant	Heraldic
294	24	Cu alloy		Scabbard	Chape
310	334	Cu alloy	Enamel	Harness pendant	Heraldic
317	69	Cu alloy		Buckle	
318	69	Cu alloy		Buckle	Pin
319	69	Cu alloy		Crotal	Large bell
377	12	Fe		Spur?	Bridle bit?
504	199	Cu alloy		Scabbard?	Dagger chape?
881	30	Cu alloy		Buckle	
898	26	Cu alloy		Buckle	
1324	188	Cu alloy		Strap fitting	Elliptical

Find No.	Field No.	Primary Material	Sub Material	Primary Type	Sub Type
1496	69	Cu alloy	Au	Harness pendant	French fleur-de-lis
1497	69	Cu alloy		Strap end	Middle section
1498	69	Cu alloy		Hooked tag	
1499	69	Cu alloy		Harness pendant	Square
1515	30	Cu alloy	Au	Mount	Square plate with gilding
1612	30	Cu alloy		Buckle	
1835	30	Cu alloy		Buckle	
1842	30	Cu alloy		Buckle	One-piece-type fragment
2221	403	Cu alloy		Buckle	
2231	100	Cu alloy		Strap fitting?	Circular
2232	181	Cu alloy		Strap end	Or scabbard fitting
2235	93	Cu alloy	Wood	Ferrule	chape
2344	569	Cu alloy		Buckle	
2360	414	Cu alloy		Buckle	
2666	187	Cu alloy		Buckle	
2713	187	Cu alloy		Buckle	
2973	706	Cu alloy		Crotal	Bell
2993	200	Cu alloy		Buckle	
3065	187	Cu alloy		Strap fitting	Belt mount
3366	402	Cu alloy		Buckle	
3561	103	Cu alloy	Ag	Strap fitting	Horse harness?
3575	103	Cu alloy		Mount	Cruciform
3576	103	Cu alloy		Strap end?	
3577	103	Cu alloy		Ring	Horse harness?
3591	95	Cu alloy		Dagger?	Rondel?
3592	181	Cu alloy	Enamel	Harness pendant	
3971	82	Pb alloy		Badge?	
4029	69	Cu alloy		Buckle	
4131	58	Cu alloy		Knife	Handle, part
4133	58	Pb alloy		Cutlery	Handle
4135	58	Pb		Weight?	Unofficial
4136	58	Cu alloy		Unidentified object	
4137	58	Cu alloy		Key	Watch
4139	58	Cu alloy		Unidentified object	
4140	58	Pb alloy		Unidentified object	

Find No.	Field No.	Primary Material	Sub Material	Primary Type	Sub Type
4175	80	Cu alloy	Sn	Rowel spur	
4220	80	Cu alloy		Buckle	
4324	81	Au		Finger ring	
4438	82	Cu alloy		Mount	Horse harness
4462	735	Cu alloy		Buckle	Spectacle
4509	46	Cu alloy	Fe	Buckle	Small spectacle
4514	46	Cu alloy		Strap end	
4575	46	Cu alloy		Buckle	Annular; pin
4648	387	Pb		Roundshot	Roundshot, 53mm diameter
4659	59	Ag		Coin	Double patard
4733	398	Pb	Fe	Roundshot	Roundshot, 47mm diameter
4734	398	Pb	Fe and flint shards	Roundshot	Roundshot, 60mm diameter
4735	398	Pb	Flint shards	Roundshot	Roundshot, 57mm diameter
4736	398	Pb		Roundshot	Roundshot, 23mm diameter
4737	206	Pb		Roundshot	Roundshot, 30mm diameter
4738	397	Pb		Roundshot	Roundshot, 35mm diameter
4752	399	Cu alloy		Buckle	Forked spacer fragment
4755	399	Cu alloy		Scabbard	Chape
4786	399	Pb		Roundshot	Roundshot, 21mm diameter
4825	542	Ag		Coin	Groat
4836	542	Cu alloy		Harness pendant?	Possible loop fragment
4886	542	Pb	Fe	Roundshot	Roundshot, 50mm diameter
4889	542	Pb		Roundshot	Roundshot, 42mm diameter
4918	30	Ag		Coin	Double patard
4919	30	Ag		Coin	Double patard
5142	548	Cu alloy	Fe	Buckle	Double looped with plate
5220	548	Cu alloy		Buckle	

Find No.	Field No.	Primary Material	Sub Material	Primary Type	Sub Type
5222	548	Pb alloy		Scabbard	Chape
5227	548	Ag	Au	Badge	Ricardian boar
5250	548	Pb		Roundshot	Roundshot, 28mm diameter
5263	549	Cu alloy		Strap fitting	
5297	542	Pb		Roundshot	Roundshot, 20mm diameter
5303	542	Pb		Roundshot	Roundshot, 44mm diameter
5305	542	Pb	Flint chunks	Roundshot	Roundshot, 56mm diameter
5321	548	Pb		Roundshot	Roundshot, 35mm diameter
5338	548	Cu alloy		Strap fitting	
5359	548	Pb		Bullet	Ball
5365	548	Pb	Stone	Roundshot	Roundshot, 97mm diameter
5385	548	Pb		Roundshot	Roundshot, 39mm diameter
5386	548	Pb		Roundshot	Roundshot, 37mm diameter
5390	548	Pb	Flint	Roundshot	Roundshot, 38mm diameter
5427	547	Pb		Roundshot	Roundshot, 38mm diameter
5428	547	Pb	Flint	Roundshot	Roundshot, 37mm diameter
5430	547	Cu alloy		Scabbard	Strapend?
5443	545	Pb		Roundshot	Roundshot, 59.5mm diameter
5465	547	Pb alloy		Buckle	
5477	547	Cu alloy		Buckle	Pin
5478	547	Cu alloy		Strap fitting	
5484	547	Pb	Flint pebble	Roundshot	Roundshot, 57mm diameter
5513	540	Pb		Roundshot	Roundshot, 35mm diameter
5541	403	Cu alloy		Buckle	
5560	556	Pb	Fe	Roundshot	Roundshot, 36mm diameter
5567	553	Cu alloy		Buckle	Double

Find No.	Field No.	Primary Material	Sub Material	Primary Type	Sub Type
5569	553	Cu alloy		Buckle	
5577	546	Cu alloy		Strap fitting	Mount
5589	546	Pb	Flint	Roundshot	Roundshot, 38mm diameter
5604	547	Cu alloy	Au	Sword	Quillon fragment
5613	547	Pb		Roundshot	Roundshot, 35mm diameter
5619	547	Pb	Flint shards	Roundshot	Roundshot, 37mm diameter
5630	547	Cu alloy		Badge?	Or mount
5649	547	Cu alloy		Harness pendant	Composite
5657	546	Cu alloy		Unidentified object	Hinge?
5678	546	Pb		Roundshot	Roundshot, 44mm diameter
5685	702	Pb	Stone pebble	Roundshot	Roundshot, 63mm diameter
5718	854	Pb alloy	Fe	Roundshot	Roundshot, 50mm diameter
5729	387	Pb alloy	Fe	Roundshot	Roundshot, 43mm diameter
5753	547	Cu alloy		Strap fitting	Rose
5761	547	Cu alloy		Spur	Rowel
5992	550	Pb		Roundshot	Roundshot, 65mm diameter
5995	550	Pb	Stone pebble	Roundshot	Roundshot, 37mm diameter
7087	1563	Pb		Roundshot	Roundshot, 40mm diameter
7127	1563	Ag		Coin	
7128	1562	Cu alloy		Dagger	Quillon
7162	1571	Pb		Mount	Star Sir John Mordaunt
7210	206	Pb	Flint shards	Roundshot	Roundshot, 58mm diameter
7211	206	Pb		Roundshot	Roundshot, 30mm diameter
7213	206	Pb		Roundshot	Roundshot, 43mm diameter
7221	206	Pb		Roundshot	Roundshot, 42mm diameter

Find No.	Field No.	Primary Material	Sub Material	Primary Type	Sub Type
7231	387	Pb	Stone pebble	Roundshot	Roundshot, 97mm diameter
7243	206	Pb		Roundshot	Roundshot, 30.5mm diameter
7252	398	Pb		Roundshot	Roundshot, 22.5mm diameter
7282	721	Pb		Roundshot	Roundshot, 40mm diameter

A List from the Bosworth Finds Classed as Possible Battle Finds

A list of 232 finds (including 18 lead balls measuring between 18mm and 20mm) extracted from the Bosworth Finds Database for recorded finds that are probably Possible Battle Finds, as of January 2021.

Find No.	Field No.	Primary Material	Sub Material	Primary Type	Sub Type
53	63	Cu alloy	Au	Mount	
56	98	Cu alloy		Stud	Spiked
89	149	Cu alloy		Buckle	Plate
116	68	Ag		Coin	Penny
119	80	Cu alloy	Fe	Strap fitting	Horse harness mount
158	80	Cu alloy		Stud	Spiked
208	178	Cu alloy		Stud	Spiked
254	186	Cu alloy		Stud	Spiked
258	187	Cu alloy		Buckle	
260	181	Pb		Button	Shanked, flower
262	181	Cu alloy		Button	
268	181	Pb alloy		Bell	Horse harness?
270	181	Cu alloy		Harness pendant?	Harness decoration
272	181	Cu alloy		Buckle or rivet	
275	181	Cu alloy		Buckle	
276	181	Cu alloy		Strap fitting	Belt slide
291	49	Cu alloy	Fe	Stud	Riveted?
292	49	Cu alloy		Harness ring?	Cast
295	24	Cu alloy		Buckle	Plate
300	24	Cu alloy		Harness ring?	
301	24	Cu alloy		Harness ring?	
308	82	Cu alloy		Stud	Spiked
311	362	Cu alloy	Fe	Stud	Riveted
496	800	Cu alloy		Dagger?	Rondel?

Find No.	Field No.	Primary Material	Sub Material	Primary Type	Sub Type
802	30	Cu alloy		Strap end	Composite, or buckle plate
805	30	Fe		Bridle fitting?	Intricately shaped rod
1162	69	Cu alloy		Stud	Spiked
1173	67	Cu alloy		Harness ring?	
1175	67	Cu alloy	Fe	Stud	Riveted
1188	67	Cu alloy		Stud	Spiked
1195	67	Cu alloy		Mount?	
1212	66	Cu alloy		Stud	Spiked
1225	69	Cu alloy	Fe	Stud	Riveted
1493	95	Cu alloy		Strap fitting	
1505	30	Cu alloy		Harness ring?	Cast
1634	30	Ag		Coin	Long-cross penny
1719	30	Cu alloy		Ring	
1865	30	Cu alloy		Ring	Cast
1871	30	Cu alloy		Ring	Cast
1968	30	Cu alloy		Harness ring?	
2229	100	Cu alloy		Harness ring?	
2358	414	Ag		Coin	Penny
2385	403	Ag		Coin	Penny
2400	97	Cu alloy		Strap fitting	
2401	97	Cu alloy		Mount	
2432	552	Cu alloy		Ring	
2446	552	Cu alloy		Stud	Spiked
2458	559	Cu alloy		Stud	Spiked
2977	571	Ag		Coin	Penny
2985	569	Cu alloy		Stud	Spiked
3337	706	Pb		Button?	
3385	100	Cu alloy		Harness ring	
3399	100	Cu alloy	Fe	Stud	Head
3556	103	Ag		Coin	Long-cross penny
3763	30	Cu alloy		Button	
3800	30	Cu alloy		Ring	Harness?
4157	765	Cu alloy		Button	
4176	80	Cu alloy		Mount	
4179	79	Cu alloy		Harness ring	
4183	79	Cu alloy		Stud	Spiked

Find No.	Field No.	Primary Material	Sub Material	Primary Type	Sub Type
4184	79	Ag		Coin	Half groat
4240	80	Cu alloy		Button	
4317	81	Cu alloy		Harness ring?	Cast
4398	82	Ag		Coin	Penny
4444	82	Pb alloy		Button	
4483	46	Cu alloy		Unidentified object	
4519	46	Cu alloy		Stud	Spiked
4526	46	Cu alloy		Ring	
4529	46	Cu alloy		Ring	
4582	46	Cu alloy	Sn	Unidentified object	
4635	226	Cu alloy		Strap fitting	Belt mount
4637	112	Cu alloy		Harness ring	Oval sectioned
4638	112	Cu alloy		Harness ring	Large
4640	112	Cu alloy		Harness ring	
4642	112	Cu alloy	Sn	Mount	
4643	112	Pb alloy		Stud	
4645	206	Cu alloy		Button	Or stud
4730	398	Ag		Coin	Farthing
4745	399	Au		Finger ring	
4754	399	Cu alloy		Stud	Spiked
4756	399	Cu alloy		Mount	Buckle plate?
4801	399	Ag		Coin	Penny
4815	542	Cu alloy		Strap fitting	
4883	399	Ag		Coin	Penny
4892	399	Cu alloy	Fe	Unidentified object	Buckle plate?
4900	30	Cu alloy		Hooked tag?	
4947	402	Cu alloy		Harness ring	
4961	402	Cu alloy	Fe	Thimble?	Flattened, or chape
5209	30	Ag		Coin	Penny, York
5238	548	Pb alloy		Purse mount?	
5251	548	Fe		Horse bit?	
5260	549	Cu Alloy		Harness ring	
5282	398	Cu alloy		Mount	Riveted
5286	398	Cu alloy	Fe	Strap end?	Or mount
5293	398	Fe		Hook	Harness fitting?
5301	542	Pb alloy		Double buckle	

Find No.	Field No.	Primary Material	Sub Material	Primary Type	Sub Type
5352	548	Cu alloy	Fe	Stud	
5382	548	Cu alloy		Stud	Spiked
5396	548	Cu alloy		Unidentified object	
5399	548	Pb alloy		Badge?	Lombardic h?
5400	548	Cu alloy		Harness fitting?	Rondell
5406	403	Cu alloy		Unidentified object	
5421	403	Cu alloy		Harness ring	Oval section
5439	547	Cu alloy		Harness ring	Oval section
5442	545	Pb alloy		Seal matrix	Pendant
5461	545	Cu alloy		Ring	Suspension, oval section
5468	547	Fe		Buckler??	Or hub
5482	547	Cu alloy		Harness buckle	
5483	547	Cu alloy	Fe	Strap fitting	Domed mount
5489	547	Cu alloy		Harness ring	
5506	547	Cu alloy	Fe	Stud	Shanked
5590	546	Pb alloy		Mount	Or stud circular
5592	546	Cu alloy		Rivet	
5594	546	Cu alloy	Ag or Sn	Strap fitting	Stud
5598	546	Pb		Inkwell	
5600	546	Cu alloy		Strap fitting?	
5610	547	Ag		Coin	Penny
5614	547	Cu alloy		Unidentified object	Hinge?
5626	547	Cu alloy		Strap end	Folded and plain
5634	547	Cu alloy		Spur fragment?	Stud fragment
5645	547	Cu alloy		Rivet	Fragment
5650	547	Pb alloy		Unidentified object	Strap end
5673	546	Cu alloy	Ag	Unidentified object	
5683	702	Ag		Coin	Penny
5692	702	Cu alloy		Buckle?	Horse harness?, asymmetric
5703	554	Cu alloy	Ag	Mount or stud?	Fragment
5706	554	Ag		Coin	Penny
5722	776	Cu alloy		Bridle?	Bit?
5725	226	Pb alloy		Scabbard?	Chape? or knife handle
5726	226	Cu alloy		Stud	

Find No.	Field No.	Primary Material	Sub Material	Primary Type	Sub Type
5732	226	Cu alloy		Mount	
5751	547	Cu alloy		Unidentified object	
5778	547	Cu alloy		Unidentified object	Cylinder with rivet
5784	100	Cu alloy		Harness ring	
5793	100	Cu alloy		Mount	Elliptical
5804	542	Cu alloy		Strap fitting?	Cruciform?
5811	542	Cu alloy		Mount	Rose
5979	539	Cu alloy	Fe	Stud	Spiked?
6211	1107	Cu alloy	Fe	Knife	Pommel
6344	1115	Cu alloy		Purse frame	
6408	1098	Cu alloy	Fe	Knife	Pommel
6429	1101	Cu alloy		Buckle	Fragment
6430	1115	Cu alloy		Buckle?	Plate?
6517	1084	Cu alloy		Harness ring	
6662	1120	Ag		Coin	Penny
6666	1116	Cu alloy		Purse frame	Fragment
7132	1571	Pb alloy	Enamel?	Button	
7141	1571	Cu alloy		Buckle	Double
7142	1571	Cu alloy	Au	Harness mount?	
7167	1571	Pb alloy		Buckle	Circular
7176	1571	Cu alloy		Belt fitting	Elliptical mount
7184	1571	Cu alloy		Mount	
3518	414	Cu alloy		Stud?	Spiked
3519	414	Cu alloy	Fe	Stud	Riveted
378	95	Fe		Spur?	
549	69	Cu alloy		Rivet	
580	69	Cu alloy		Harness ring?	Cast
235	67	Cu alloy		Harness ring?	
4196	67	Cu alloy		Stud	Spiked
518	81	Cu alloy		Stud	Spiked
3512	571	Cu alloy		Stud	Spiked?, no spike
3201	65	Cu alloy		Stud	Spiked
7228	206			Cutlery	Handle
1377	200	Cu alloy		Stud	Spiked
3491	197	Cu alloy		Knife	Pommel
958	52	Pb alloy		Button	
667	43	Cu alloy		Harness ring?	

Find No.	Field No.	Primary Material	Sub Material	Primary Type	Sub Type
1468	324	Pb	Fe	Button	
1469	324	Fe		Buckle	Horse harness
2112	329	Pb		Button?	
1423	329	Cu alloy		Stud	Riveted
348	329	Cu alloy		Strap fitting	Elliptical
1414	329	Cu alloy		Harness ring?	
1421	329	Pb alloy		Button?	Small
350	328	Pb		Badge?	Rose
2099	330	Cu alloy		Stud	Riveted
2176	13	Cu alloy		Harness ring?	Cast
2748	160	Cu alloy		Stud	Spiked
376	31	Fe		Spur?	Arm?
1320	188	Ag		Coin	Penny
1332	188	Cu alloy		Button	
1120	186	Cu alloy		Stud	Spiked
2665	187	Ag		Coin	Penny
3086	187	Cu alloy		Harness ring?	
3087	187	Cu alloy		Harness ring?	
3107	187	Cu alloy		Stud	Spiked
3492	187	Cu alloy		Button	
705	43	Cu alloy	Fe	Stud	Riveted
710	43	Cu alloy		Stud	Spiked
726	43	Cu alloy		Stud	Riveted
333	181	Cu alloy		Strap fitting	Elliptical
334	181	Cu alloy		Strap end	Ball
338	181	Cu alloy		Strap fitting	Elliptical
339	181	Pb		Button?	
2491	181	Cu alloy		Ring	Round-sectioned
820	30	Cu alloy		Ring	Chainmail?
831	30	Cu alloy		Harness ring	
835	30	Cu alloy		Stud	Spiked
2546	181	Cu alloy		Unidentified object	
2909	294	Cu alloy		Ring	Horse harness
7280	721	Cu alloy		Belt hanger	Double-loop oval
7380	721	Cu Alloy		Buckle	Whithead 570
7506	201	Ag		Coin	
7587	729	Cu alloy		Purse bar	

Find No.	Field No.	Primary Material	Sub Material	Primary Type	Sub Type
7608	198	Cu alloy		Fitting	Bridle
7627	379	Cu alloy		Fitting	Bridle
7649	379	Cu alloy		Fitting	Bridle
7660	379	Cu alloy		Plate	Belt
7661	379	Cu alloy		Fitting	Strap
7666	379	Cu alloy		Fitting	Bridle
7695	202	Cu alloy		Button	
7703	202	Cu alloy		Buckle	
7707	202	Cu alloy		Button	
7725	271	Ag		Coin	Med
1424	329	Pb		Bullet	Ball, 20.34mm diameter
5974	852	Pb		Bullet	Ball, 19.89mm diameter
7457	553	Pb		Bullet	Ball, 19.3mm dia
5258	549	Pb		Bullet	Ball, 19mm diameter
5413	403	Cu alloy		Bullet	Ball, 18.79mm diameter
299	24	Pb		Bullet	Ball, 18.58mm diameter
5410	403	Pb		Bullet	Ball, 18.48mm diameter
2500	181	Pb		Bullet	Ball, 18.4mm dia
297	24	Pb		Bullet	Ball, 18.05mm diameter
5274	549	Pb	Fe	Bullet	Ball, 18mm diameter
7230	387	Pb		Bullet	Ball, 18mm diameter
7310	721	Pb		Bullet	Ball, 18mm diameter
7473	198	Pb		Bullet	Ball, 18mm diameter
7497	201	Pb		Bullet	Ball, 18mm diameter
7502	201	Pb		Bullet	Ball, 18mm diameter
7525	201	Pb		Bullet	Ball, 18mm diameter
7696	202	Pb		Bullet	Ball, 18mm diameter
7716	202	Pb		Bullet	Ball, 18mm diameter

Appendix IV

Lists of 'Lead Spheres' over 7g in Weight or 12mm in Diameter

A list of 310 finds extracted from the Bosworth Finds Database for recorded finds that are some form of 'lead sphere', as of January 2021.

Find No.	Field No.	Main Material	Sub Material	Main Type	Sub Type	Weight grams	Size mm
58	98	Pb		Bullet	Ball	14.17	13.75
91	149	Pb		Bullet	Ball	21.90	15.77
112	68	Pb		Bullet	Ball	10.67	12.72
120	80	Pb		Bullet		7.08	7.74
196	178	Pb		Bullet	Ball	18.34	14.53
243	95	Pb		Bullet		7.72	8.93
297	24	Pb		Bullet	Ball	30.72	18.05
298	24	Pb		Bullet	Ball	22.77	16.61
299	24	Pb		Bullet	Ball	33.84	18.58
331	82	Pb		Bullet	Ball	1.81	6.84
357	15	Pb		Bullet	Ball	15.90	14.52
384	13	Pb		Bullet	Ball	8.95	12.70
388	13	Pb		Bullet		4.64	7.52
392	82	Pb		Bullet	Ball	11.03	13.54
393	82	Pb		Bullet	x 3	5.13	7.72
486	49	Pb		Bullet	Ball	17.99	15.64
551	69	Pb		Bullet	Ball	7.39	12.07
552	69	Pb		Bullet	Ball	7.49	11.38
576	69	Pb		Bullet		4.19	7.41
638	53	Pb		Bullet		7.14	9.33
658	43	Pb		Bullet	Ball	12.08	13.04
796	30	Pb		Bullet	Ball, large	22.42	16.22
845	30	Pb		Bullet	Ball	13.67	13.80
855	30	Pb		Bullet		4.74	7.53
857	30	Pb		Bullet	Ball	20.49	16.05

Find No.	Field No.	Main Material	Sub Material	Main Type	Sub Type	Weight grams	Size mm
861	30	Pb		Bullet	Ball	2.52	9.54
894	26	Pb		Bullet	Ball	12.72	13.65
963	52	Pb		Bullet	Ball	7.15	11.02
964	52	Pb		Bullet	Ball	7.26	11.28
1179	67	Pb		Bullet	Impacted	0.00	0.00
1217	66	Pb		Bullet	Ball	5.97	11.25
1245	67	Pb		Bullet		5.04	7.47
1246	67	Pb		Bullet		4.95	7.50
1279	199	Pb		Bullet	Ball	9.25	12.77
1286	199	Pb		Bullet	Ball	5.77	10.73
1343	188	Pb		Bullet	Ball	11.72	12.98
1347	188	Pb		Bullet	Ball	9.30	13.52
1356	188	Pb		Bullet	Ball	9.74	12.85
1379	200	Pb		Bullet	Ball	9.40	12.46
1389	327	Pb		Bullet	Ball	9.24	12.27
1390	327	Pb		Bullet	Ball	19.96	17.12
1400	327	Pb		Bullet	Ball	8.14	11.69
1402	327	Pb		Bullet	Ball	12.66	13.66
1416	329	Pb		Bullet	Ball	15.66	15.12
1424	329	Pb		Bullet	Ball	25.03	20.34
1517	30	Pb		Bullet	Ball	0.00	0.00
1526	30	Pb		Bullet	Ball	0.00	0.00
1859	30	Pb		Bullet	Ball	0.00	0.00
1998	30	Pb		Bullet	Ball	3.37	8.32
2057	30	Pb		Bullet		6.78	9.30
2058	30	Pb		Bullet		7.46	9.15
2097	330	Pb		Bullet		2.51	5.76
2118	329	Pb		Bullet	Ball	17.33	0.00
2122	329	Pb		Bullet		2.59	5.84
2278	404	Pb		Bullet	Ball	3.22	8.73
2304	82	Pb		Bullet	Ball	15.05	16.61
2305	13	Pb		Bullet	Ball	10.67	13.35
2418	550	Pb		Bullet	Ball	18.30	15.44
2423	554	Pb		Bullet	Ball	17.38	15.36
2456	559	Pb		Bullet	Ball	3.49	8.92
2495	181	Pb		Bullet	Ball	9.46	12.73
2496	181	Pb		Bullet	Ball	9.22	12.51

Find No.	Field No.	Main Material	Sub Material	Main Type	Sub Type	Weight grams	Size mm
2497	181	Pb		Bullet	Ball	17.88	15.14
2498	181	Pb		Bullet	Ball	11.53	13.59
2499	181	Pb		Bullet	Ball	19.68	15.19
2500	181	Pb		Bullet	Ball	28.83	18.40
2501	181	Pb		Bullet	Ball	14.43	14.10
2502	181	Pb		Bullet	Ball	8.99	13.06
2503	181	Pb		Bullet	Ball	11.56	12.79
2504	181	Pb		Bullet	Ball	8.60	12.16
2505	181	Pb		Bullet	Ball	11.20	13.93
2506	181	Pb		Bullet	Ball	13.61	13.73
2507	181	Pb		Bullet	Ball	11.52	13.84
2508	181	Pb		Bullet	Ball	11.70	13.86
2509	181	Pb		Bullet	Ball	14.56	13.43
2510	181	Pb		Bullet	Ball	9.43	12.70
2511	181	Pb		Bullet	Ball	9.99	12.22
2512	181	Pb		Bullet	Ball	10.90	13.41
2513	181	Pb		Bullet	Ball	10.02	11.81
2514	181	Pb		Bullet	Ball	11.09	13.77
2515	181	Pb		Bullet	Ball	9.19	12.30
2516	181	Pb		Bullet	Ball	8.84	12.16
2517	181	Pb		Bullet	Ball	9.35	12.58
2518	181	Pb		Bullet	Ball	11.07	13.42
2519	181	Pb		Bullet	Ball	7.95	11.48
2520	181	Pb		Bullet	Ball	6.47	11.35
2521	181	Pb		Bullet	Ball	8.70	11.88
2522	181	Pb		Bullet	Ball	5.70	10.72
2523	181	Pb		Bullet	Ball	7.79	11.33
2524	181	Pb		Bullet	Ball	7.45	11.15
2525	181	Pb		Bullet	Ball	2.70	7.93
2526	181	Pb		Bullet	Ball	2.62	8.82
2527	181	Pb		Bullet	Ball	3.28	9.40
2576	174	Pb		Bullet	Ball	7.85	11.88
2577	174	Pb		Bullet	Ball	14.79	13.83
2578	181	Pb		Bullet	Ball	9.49	12.88
2842	95	Pb		Bullet	Ball	30.32	17.26
2845	95	Pb		Bullet	Ball	15.68	14.47
2851	95	Pb		Bullet		0.00	0.00

Find No.	Field No.	Main Material	Sub Material	Main Type	Sub Type	Weight grams	Size mm
2886	193	Pb		Bullet	Ball	10.08	12.28
2887	193	Pb		Bullet	Ball	20.25	15.05
2919	294	Pb		Bullet	Ball	9.09	11.80
2920	297	Pb		Bullet	Ball	25.19	16.00
2948	296	Pb		Bullet		4.90	7.40
2972	579	Pb		Bullet	Ball	6.82	10.46
2976	571	Pb		Bullet	Ball	4.47	9.80
2980	557	Pb		Bullet	Ball	13.16	14.00
2984	569	Pb		Bullet	Ball	7.71	11.35
2987	569	Pb		Bullet	Ball	16.77	14.58
2989	846	Pb		Bullet	Ball	10.69	12.49
3026	30	Pb		Bullet		7.63	8.99
3052	187	Pb		Bullet	Ball	25.96	17.00
3054	187	Pb		Bullet	Ball	19.67	15.00
3055	187	Pb		Bullet	Ball	15.25	14.00
3203	181	Pb		Bullet	Ball	14.48	14.53
3294	30	Pb		Bullet	Impacted	2.18	0.00
3388	69	Pb		Bullet		0.00	0.00
3422	93	Pb		Bullet	Ball	16.71	14.78
3532	70	Pb		Bullet	Ball	11.75	13.19
3569	103	Pb		Bullet	Ball	8.32	11.77
3583	103	Pb		Bullet	Ball	29.64	17.62
3730	30	Pb		Bullet		7.45	4.23
3741	30	Pb		Bullet		7.46	9.50
3752	30	Pb		Bullet		0.00	0.00
3754	30	Pb		Bullet		0.00	0.00
3797	30	Pb		Bullet		0.00	0.00
3839	30	Pb		Bullet		0.00	0.00
3844	30	Pb		Bullet		0.00	0.00
3856	30	Pb		Bullet	Ball	6.60	10.53
3947	30	Pb alloy		Bullet		0.00	0.00
4022	69	Pb		Bullet		0.00	0.00
4030	69	Pb alloy		Bullet	Ball	6.57	10.74
4097	69	Pb		Bullet	Ball	6.56	11.41
4116	88	Pb		Bullet	Ball	7.10	14.34
4205	108	Pb		Bullet	Ball	14.56	14.90
4212	80	Pb		Bullet	Impacted	7.12	0.00

Find No.	Field No.	Main Material	Sub Material	Main Type	Sub Type	Weight grams	Size mm
4284	30	Pb		Bullet	Ball	8.21	11.70
4287	30	Pb		Bullet		0.00	0.00
4304	549	Pb		Bullet	Ball	6.78	10.55
4315	81	Pb		Bullet	Ball	13.47	13.53
4347	82	Pb		Bullet	Ball	2.10	7.37
4366	239	Pb		Bullet	Ball	18.18	15.03
4367	239	Pb		Bullet	Ball	18.79	14.49
4368	239	Pb alloy?		Bullet	Ball	22.37	15.87
4413	65	Pb		Bullet	Ball	17.32	15.10
4427	65	Pb		Bullet	Impacted	0.00	0.00
4435	65	Pb		Bullet	Ball	6.70	11.99
4447	82	Pb		Bullet	Ball	7.01	10.77
4507	46	Pb		Bullet	Ball	9.04	11.61
4511	46	Pb		Bullet	Ball, impacted	8.10	11.34
4512	46	Pb		Bullet	Ball, impacted	7.98	11.63
4515	46	Pb		Bullet	Ball, large	35.71	18.65
4516	46	Pb		Bullet	Ball	4.09	9.49
4537	46	Pb		Bullet	Ball	8.49	11.52
4538	46	Pb		Bullet	Ball	7.05	10.83
4543	46	Pb		Bullet	Ball, offset	6.39	11.43
4548	46	Pb		Bullet	Ball	20.73	15.35
4572	46	Pb		Bullet	Ball	14.54	13.98
4576	46	Pb		Bullet	Ball	4.30	9.15
4578	46	Pb		Bullet	Ball	4.55	9.43
4579	46	Pb		Bullet	Ball, large	36.19	18.61
4581	46	Pb		Bullet	Ball	9.20	12.14
4592	226	Pb		Bullet	Ball, impacted	3.38	8.55
4593	206	Pb		Bullet	Ball, miscast	20.10	16.19
4594	206	Pb		Bullet	Ball	16.00	14.62
4646	206	Pb		Bullet	Ball	20.89	14.86
4648	387	Pb		Shot	Roundshot	911.00	53.00
4660	206	Pb		Bullet	Ball	20.85	15.14
4733	398	Pb	Fe	Shot	Roundshot	452.00	47.00
4734	398	Pb	Fe and flint shards	Shot	Roundshot	906.00	60.00

Find No.	Field No.	Main Material	Sub Material	Main Type	Sub Type	Weight grams	Size mm
4735	398	Pb	Flint shards	Shot	Roundshot	793.00	57.00
4736	398	Pb		Shot	Roundshot	70.00	23.00
4737	206	Pb		Shot	Roundshot	159.00	30.00
4738	397	Pb		Shot	Roundshot	260.00	35.00
4739	398			Bullet	Ball, small calibre	19.65	14.92
4786	399	Pb		Shot	Roundshot	52.00	21.00
4816	542	Pb		Bullet	Ball	23.99	17.05
4876	399	Pb		Bullet	Ball	8.10	11.74
4886	542	Pb	Fe	Shot	Roundshot	656.00	50.00
4889	542	Pb		Shot	Roundshot	405.00	42.00
4932	399	Pb		Bullet	Impacted	1.86	0.00
4939	399	Pb		Bullet	Ball	10.13	12.61
4946	402	Pb		Bullet	Ball	2.13	9.99
4968	402	Pb		Bullet	Ball	10.01	12.48
4995	30	Pb		Bullet	Ball	8.33	11.52
5019	80	Pb		Bullet	Ball	15.18	14.18
5158	548	Pb		Bullet	Ball	13.17	12.97
5170	548	Pb		Bullet	Ball	13.37	13.44
5179	548	Pb		Bullet	Ball	13.35	13.10
5250	548	Pb		Shot	Roundshot	125.00	28.00
5254	549	Pb		Bullet	Ball	6.00	10.50
5258	549	Pb		Bullet	Ball	30.00	19.00
5261	549	Pb		Bullet	Ball	6.00	10.00
5274	549	Pb	Fe	Bullet	Ball	21.00	18.00
5290	398	Pb		Bullet	Ball	7.68	11.21
5297	542	Pb		Shot	Rroundshot	53.00	20.00
5303	542	Pb		Shot	Roundshot	486.00	44.00
5305	542	Pb	Flint chunks	Shot	Roundshot	760.00	56.00
5321	548	Pb		Shot	Roundshot	254.00	35.00
5334	548	Pb		Bullet	Ball	7.32	10.82
5359	548	Pb		Bullet	Ball	26.65	17.29
5365	548	Pb	Stone	Shot	Roundshot	3,214.00	97.00
5385	548	Pb		Shot	Roundshot	262.00	39.00
5386	548	Pb		Shot	Roundshot	295.00	37.00
5390	548	Pb	Flint	Shot	Roundshot	254.00	38.00

Find No.	Field No.	Main Material	Sub Material	Main Type	Sub Type	Weight grams	Size mm
5410	403	Pb		Bullet	Ball	35.40	18.48
5413	403	Cu alloy		Bullet	Ball	1.02	18.79
5424	547	Pb		Bullet	Ball	15.98	14.77
5427	547	Pb		Shot	Roundshot	306.00	38.00
5428	547	Pb	Flint	Shot	Roundshot	250.00	37.00
5443	545	Pb		Shot	Roundshot	925.00	59.50
5446	545	Pb		Bullet	Ball	16.08	14.30
5450	545	Pb		Bullet	Ball	8.56	12.20
5484	547	Pb	Flint pebble	Shot	Roundshot	674.00	57.00
5497	547	Pb		Bullet	Ball	12.85	13.23
5513	540	Pb		Shot	Roundshot	254.00	35.00
5518	540	Pb		Bullet	Ball	5.99	10.16
5527	547	Pb		Bullet	Ball	23.20	16.27
5531	403	Pb		Bullet	Ball	6.11	10.92
5560	556	Pb	Fe	Shot	Roundshot	244.00	36.00
5581	546	Pb		Bullet	Ball, pistol?	6.90	10.57
5589	546	Pb	Flint	Shot	Roundshot	249.00	38.00
5601	546	Pb		Bullet	Ball, pistol?	3.10	9.44
5613	547	Pb		Shot	Roundshot	251.00	35.00
5619	547	Pb	Flint shards	Shot	Roundshot	247.00	37.00
5672	546	Pb		Bullet	Ball	10.54	12.46
5678	546	Pb		Shot	Roundshot	415.00	44.00
5682	702	Pb		Bullet	Impacted	0.00	0.00
5685	702	Pb	Stone pebble	Shot	Roundshot	1,066.00	63.00
5718	854	Pb alloy	Fe	Shot	Roundshot	567.00	50.00
5729	387	Pb alloy	Fe	Shot	Roundshot	468.00	43.00
5734	545	Pb		Bullet	Ball	18.01	14.78
5742	545	Pb		Bullet	Ball	24.72	17.05
5758	547	Pb		Bullet	Ball	5.13	10.18
5768	547	Pb		Bullet	Ball	3.73	8.80
5774	547	Pb		Bullet	Ball	3.42	9.12
5776	547	Pb		Bullet	Ball	5.96	10.95
5777	547	Pb		Bullet	Ball	2.53	7.74
5782	63	Pb		Bullet	Ball	3.17	9.07

Find No.	Field No.	Main Material	Sub Material	Main Type	Sub Type	Weight grams	Size mm
5796	100	Pb		Bullet	Ball	12.51	12.70
5971	852	Pb		Bullet	Ball	12.28	13.25
5974	852	Pb		Bullet	Ball	41.05	19.89
5976	852	Pb		Bullet	Ball, pistol?	4.15	9.59
5980	539	Pb		Bullet	Ball?, impacted?	22.69	18.00
5983	539	Pb		Bullet	Ball, impacted	21.12	16.76
5992	550	Pb		Shot	Roundshot	1,127.00	65.00
5995	550	Pb	Stone pebble	Shot	Roundshot	297.00	37.00
6007	541	Pb		Bullet	Ball, wormed	18.34	14.70
6057	887	Pb		Bullet	Ball	10.13	12.68
6177	1028	Pb		Bullet	Ball, impacted	10.00	13.50
6214	1105	Pb		Bullet	Ball	25.00	17.00
6215	1105	Pb		Bullet	Ball	25.00	17.00
6321	1108	Pb		Bullet	Ball	20.00	15.50
6409	1098	Pb		Bullet	Ball	5.00	9.00
6439	1110	Pb		Bullet	Ball	25.00	16.00
6472	1118	Pb		Bullet	Ball	10.00	12.00
6498	1117	Pb		Bullet	Ball	5.00	10.00
6504	1117	Pb		Bullet	Ball	5.00	10.00
6506	1117	Pb		Bullet	Ball	10.00	11.00
6571	1164	Pb alloy		Bullet	Ball, unfinished	5.00	9.00
6575	1164	Pb		Bullet	Ball	5.00	7.00
6775	1087	Pb		bullet	Ball, impacted	15.00	14.00
6794	1087	Pb		Bullet	Ball, impacted	5.00	9.00
6857	1092	Pb		Bullet	Ball, impacted	10.00	12.00
7087	1563	Pb		Shot	Roundshot	370.00	40.00
7210	206	Pb	Flint shards	Shot	Roundshot	795.00	58.00
7211	206	Pb		Shot	Roundshot	151.60	30.00
7212	206	Pb		Bullet	Ball	21.50	15.30
7213	206	Pb		Shot	Roundshot	415.20	43.00

Find No.	Field No.	Main Material	Sub Material	Main Type	Sub Type	Weight grams	Size mm
7215	206	Pb		Bullet	Ball	24.90	16.00
7216	206	Pb		Bullet	Ball	9.60	12.60
7218	206	Pb		Bullet	Ball	11.20	12.00
7221	206	Pb		Shot	Roundshot	400.70	42.00
7222	206	Pb		Bullet	Ball, impacted	11.30	12.00
7229	206	Pb		Bullet	Ball	7.40	11.00
7230	387	Pb		Bullet	Ball	34.10	18.00
7231	387	Pb	Stone pebble	Shot	Roundshot	3,577.00	97.00
7243	206	Pb		Shot	Roundshot	161.00	30.50
7244	206	Pb		Bullet	Ball	21.50	15.00
7252	398	Pb		Shot	Roundshot	67.90	22.50
7282	721	Pb		Shot	Roundshot	411.00	40.00
7296	721	Pb		Bullet	Dome-shaped distorted	0.00	0.00
7310	721	Pb		Bullet	Ball	33.00	18.00
7329	881	Pb		Bullet	Ball	27.00	17.00
7334	721	Pb		Bullet	Ball	0.00	0.00
7357	721	Pb		Bullet	Ball	0.00	12.00
7358	721	Pb		Bullet	Ball sprue scar	0.00	8.00
7365	721	Pb		Bullet	Ball sprue scar	0.00	9.00
7397	882	Pb		Bullet	Ball base of casting	0.00	13.00
7401	886	Pb		Bullet	Ball base of casting	0.00	13.00
7440	858	Pb		Bullet	Ball	0.00	13.00
7457	553	Pb		Bullet	Ball	38.20	19.30
7460	198	Pb		Bullet	Ball	0.00	12.00
7473	198	Pb		Bullet	Ball	0.00	18.00
7497	201	Pb		Bullet	Ball	0.00	18.00
7502	201	Pb		Bullet	Ball	0.00	18.00
7525	201	Pb		Bullet	Ball	0.00	18.00
7526	201	Pb		Bullet	Ball	0.00	16.00
7527	201	Pb		Bullet	Ball	0.00	10.00
7529	201	Pb		Bullet	Ball	0.00	10.00
7574	729	Pb		Bullet	Ball	0.00	8.00

Find No.	Field No.	Main Material	Sub Material	Main Type	Sub Type	Weight grams	Size mm
7582	729	Pb		Bullet	Ball	0.00	15.00
7584	729	Pb		Bullet	Ball	0.00	8.00
7607	198	Pb		Bullet	Ball	0.00	15.00
7634	379	Pb		Bullet	Ball	0.00	8.00
7690	202	Pb		Bullet	Ball	0.00	10.00
7696	202	Pb		Bullet	Ball	0.00	18.00
7698	202	Pb		Bullet	Ball	0.00	12.00
7701	202	Pb		Bullet	Ball	0.00	12.00
7716	202	Pb		Bullet	Ball	0.00	18.00

The following list of 22 lead spheres, recorded in the researched areas and extracted from the list of 310, are in need of accurate measuring.

Find No.	Field No.	Main Material	Sub Material	Main Type	Sub Type	Weight grams	Size mm
1179	67	Pb		Bullet	Impacted	0.00	0.00
1517	30	Pb		Bullet	Ball	0.00	0.00
1526	30	Pb		Bullet	Ball	0.00	0.00
1859	30	Pb		Bullet	Ball	0.00	0.00
2118	329	Pb		Bullet	Ball, impacted	17.33	0.00
2851	95	Pb		Bullet		0.00	0.00
3294	30	Pb		Bullet	Impacted	2.18	0.00
3388	69	Pb		Bullet		0.00	0.00
3752	30	Pb		Bullet		0.00	0.00
3754	30	Pb		Bullet		0.00	0.00
3797	30	Pb		Bullet		0.00	0.00
3839	30	Pb		Bullet		0.00	0.00
3844	30	Pb		Bullet		0.00	0.00
3947	30	Pb alloy		Bullet		0.00	0.00
4022	69	Pb		Bullet		0.00	0.00
4212	80	Pb		Bullet	Impacted	7.12	0.00
4287	30	Pb		Bullet		0.00	0.00
4427	65	Pb		Bullet	Impacted	0.00	0.00
4932	399	Pb		Bullet	Impacted	1.86	0.00
5682	702	Pb		Bullet	Impacted	0.00	0.00
7296	721	Pb		Bullet	Dome-shaped distorted	0.00	0.00
7334	721	Pb		Bullet	Ball	0.00	0.00

A list of 196 lead spheres recorded in the researched areas that are potential handgunne shot (i.e. 10–20mm diameter). They have been grouped by field number.

Find No.	Field No.	Main Material	Sub Material	Main Type	Sub Type	Weight grams	Size mm
384	13	Pb		Bullet	Ball	8.95	12.70
2305	13	Pb		Bullet	Ball	10.67	13.35
357	15	Pb		Bullet	Ball	15.90	14.52
298	24	Pb		Bullet	Ball	22.77	16.61
297	24	Pb		Bullet	Ball	30.72	18.05
299	24	Pb		Bullet	Ball	33.84	18.58
894	26	Pb		Bullet	Ball	12.72	13.65
3856	30	Pb		Bullet	Ball	6.60	10.53
4995	30	Pb		Bullet	Ball	8.33	11.52
4284	30	Pb		Bullet	Ball	8.21	11.70
845	30	Pb		Bullet	Ball	13.67	13.80
857	30	Pb		Bullet	Ball	20.49	16.05
796	30	Pb		Bullet	Ball, large	22.42	16.22
658	43	Pb		Bullet	Ball	12.08	13.04
4538	46	Pb		Bullet	Ball	7.05	10.83
4511	46	Pb		Bullet	Ball, impacted	8.10	11.34
4543	46	Pb		Bullet	Ball, offset	6.39	11.43
4537	46	Pb		Bullet	Ball	8.49	11.52
4507	46	Pb		Bullet	Ball	9.04	11.61
4512	46	Pb		Bullet	Ball, impacted	7.98	11.63
4581	46	Pb		Bullet	Ball	9.20	12.14
4572	46	Pb		Bullet	Ball	14.54	13.98
4548	46	Pb		Bullet	Ball	20.73	15.35
4579	46	Pb		Bullet	Ball, large	36.19	18.61
4515	46	Pb		Bullet	Ball, large	35.71	18.65
486	49	Pb		Bullet	Ball	17.99	15.64
963	52	Pb		Bullet	Ball	7.15	11.02
964	52	Pb		Bullet	Ball	7.26	11.28
4435	65	Pb		Bullet	Ball	6.70	11.99
4413	65	Pb		Bullet	Ball	17.32	15.10
1217	66	Pb		Bullet	Ball	5.97	11.25
112	68	Pb		Bullet	Ball	10.67	12.72

Find No.	Field No.	Main Material	Sub Material	Main Type	Sub Type	Weight grams	Size mm
4030	69	Pb alloy		Bullet	Ball	6.57	10.74
552	69	Pb		Bullet	Ball	7.49	11.38
4097	69	Pb		Bullet	Ball	6.56	11.41
551	69	Pb		Bullet	Ball	7.39	12.07
3532	70	Pb		Bullet	Ball	11.75	13.19
5019	80	Pb		Bullet	Ball	15.18	14.18
4315	81	Pb		Bullet	Ball	13.47	13.53
4447	82	Pb		Bullet	Ball	7.01	10.77
392	82	Pb		Bullet	Ball	11.03	13.54
2304	82	Pb		Bullet	Ball	15.05	16.61
4116	88	Pb		Bullet	Ball	7.10	14.34
3422	93	Pb		Bullet	Ball	16.71	14.78
2845	95	Pb		Bullet	Ball	15.68	14.47
2842	95	Pb		Bullet	Ball	30.32	17.26
58	98	Pb		Bullet	Ball	14.17	13.75
5796	100	Pb		Bullet	Ball	12.51	12.70
3569	103	Pb		Bullet	Ball	8.32	11.77
3583	103	Pb		Bullet	Ball	29.64	17.62
4205	108	Pb		Bullet	Ball	14.56	14.90
91	149	Pb		Bullet	Ball	21.90	15.77
2576	174	Pb		Bullet	Ball	7.85	11.88
2577	174	Pb		Bullet	Ball	14.79	13.83
196	178	Pb		Bullet	Ball	18.34	14.53
2522	181	Pb		Bullet	Ball	5.70	10.72
2524	181	Pb		Bullet	Ball	7.45	11.15
2523	181	Pb		Bullet	Ball	7.79	11.33
2520	181	Pb		Bullet	Ball	6.47	11.35
2519	181	Pb		Bullet	Ball	7.95	11.48
2513	181	Pb		Bullet	Ball	10.02	11.81
2521	181	Pb		Bullet	Ball	8.70	11.88
2504	181	Pb		Bullet	Ball	8.60	12.16
2516	181	Pb		Bullet	Ball	8.84	12.16
2511	181	Pb		Bullet	Ball	9.99	12.22
2515	181	Pb		Bullet	Ball	9.19	12.30
2496	181	Pb		Bullet	Ball	9.22	12.51
2517	181	Pb		Bullet	Ball	9.35	12.58
2510	181	Pb		Bullet	Ball	9.43	12.70

Find No.	Field No.	Main Material	Sub Material	Main Type	Sub Type	Weight grams	Size mm
2495	181	Pb		Bullet	Ball	9.46	12.73
2503	181	Pb		Bullet	Ball	11.56	12.79
2578	181	Pb		Bullet	Ball	9.49	12.88
2502	181	Pb		Bullet	Ball	8.99	13.06
2512	181	Pb		Bullet	Ball	10.90	13.41
2518	181	Pb		Bullet	Ball	11.07	13.42
2509	181	Pb		Bullet	Ball	14.56	13.43
2498	181	Pb		Bullet	Ball	11.53	13.59
2506	181	Pb		Bullet	Ball	13.61	13.73
2514	181	Pb		Bullet	Ball	11.09	13.77
2507	181	Pb		Bullet	Ball	11.52	13.84
2508	181	Pb		Bullet	Ball	11.70	13.86
2505	181	Pb		Bullet	Ball	11.20	13.93
2501	181	Pb		Bullet	Ball	14.43	14.10
3203	181	Pb		Bullet	Ball	14.48	14.53
2497	181	Pb		Bullet	Ball	17.88	15.14
2499	181	Pb		Bullet	Ball	19.68	15.19
2500	181	Pb		Bullet	Ball	28.83	18.40
3055	187	Pb		Bullet	Ball	15.25	14.00
3054	187	Pb		Bullet	Ball	19.67	15.00
3052	187	Pb		Bullet	Ball	25.96	17.00
1356	188	Pb		Bullet	Ball	9.74	12.85
1343	188	Pb		Bullet	Ball	11.72	12.98
1347	188	Pb		Bullet	Ball	9.30	13.52
2886	193	Pb		Bullet	Ball	10.08	12.28
2887	193	Pb		Bullet	Ball	20.25	15.05
7460	198	Pb		Bullet	Ball	0.00	12.00
7607	198	Pb		Bullet	Ball	0.00	15.00
7473	198	Pb		Bullet	Ball	0.00	18.00
1286	199	Pb		Bullet	Ball	5.77	10.73
1279	199	Pb		Bullet	Ball	9.25	12.77
1379	200	Pb		Bullet	Ball	9.40	12.46
7527	201	Pb		Bullet	Ball	0.00	10.00
7529	201	Pb		Bullet	Ball	0.00	10.00
7526	201	Pb		Bullet	Ball	0.00	16.00
7497	201	Pb		Bullet	Ball	0.00	18.00
7502	201	Pb		Bullet	Ball	0.00	18.00

Find No.	Field No.	Main Material	Sub Material	Main Type	Sub Type	Weight grams	Size mm
7525	201	Pb		Bullet	Ball	0.00	18.00
7690	202	Pb		Bullet	Ball	0.00	10.00
7698	202	Pb		Bullet	Ball	0.00	12.00
7701	202	Pb		Bullet	Ball	0.00	12.00
7696	202	Pb		Bullet	Ball	0.00	18.00
7716	202	Pb		Bullet	Ball	0.00	18.00
7229	206	Pb		Bullet	Ball	7.40	11.00
7218	206	Pb		Bullet	Ball	11.20	12.00
7222	206	Pb		Bullet	Ball, impacted	11.30	12.00
7216	206	Pb		Bullet	Ball	9.60	12.60
4594	206	Pb		Bullet	Ball	16.00	14.62
4646	206	Pb		Bullet	Ball	20.89	14.86
7244	206	Pb		Bullet	Ball	21.50	15.00
4660	206	Pb		Bullet	Ball	20.85	15.14
7212	206	Pb		Bullet	Ball	21.50	15.30
7215	206	Pb		Bullet	Ball	24.90	16.00
4593	206	Pb		Bullet	Ball, miscast	20.10	16.19
4367	239	Pb		Bullet	Ball	18.79	14.49
4366	239	Pb		Bullet	Ball	18.18	15.03
4368	239	Pb alloy?		Bullet	Ball	22.37	15.87
2919	294	Pb		Bullet	Ball	9.09	11.80
2920	297	Pb		Bullet	Ball	25.19	16.00
1400	327	Pb		Bullet	Ball	8.14	11.69
1389	327	Pb		Bullet	Ball	9.24	12.27
1402	327	Pb		Bullet	Ball	12.66	13.66
1390	327	Pb		Bullet	Ball	19.96	17.12
1416	329	Pb		Bullet	Ball	15.66	15.12
7230	387	Pb		Bullet	Ball	34.10	18.00
5290	398	Pb		Bullet	Ball	7.68	11.21
4739	398	Pb		Bullet	Ball, small calibre	19.65	14.92
4876	399	Pb		Bullet	Ball	8.10	11.74
4939	399	Pb		Bullet	Ball	10.13	12.61
4968	402	Pb		Bullet	Ball	10.01	12.48
5531	403	Pb		Bullet	Ball	6.11	10.92
5410	403	Pb		Bullet	Ball	35.40	18.48

Find No.	Field No.	Main Material	Sub Material	Main Type	Sub Type	Weight grams	Size mm
5983	539	Pb		Bullet	Ball, impacted	21.12	16.76
5980	539	Pb		Bullet	Ball?, impacted?	22.69	18.00
5518	540	Pb		Ball	Ball	5.99	10.16
6007	541	Pb		Bullet	Ball, wormed	18.34	14.70
4816	542	Pb		Bullet	Ball	23.99	17.05
5450	545	Pb		Bullet	Ball	8.56	12.20
5446	545	Pb		Bullet	Ball	16.08	14.30
5734	545	Pb		Bullet	Ball	18.01	14.78
5742	545	Pb		Bullet	Ball	24.72	17.05
5581	546	Pb		Bullet	Ball, pistol?	6.90	10.57
5672	546	Pb		Bullet	Ball	10.54	12.46
5758	547	Pb		Bullet	Ball	5.13	10.18
5776	547	Pb		Bullet	Ball	5.96	10.95
5497	547	Pb		Bullet	Ball	12.85	13.23
5424	547	Pb		Bullet	Ball	15.98	14.77
5527	547	Pb		Bullet	Ball	23.20	16.27
5334	548	Pb		Bullet	Ball	7.32	10.82
5158	548	Pb		Bullet	Ball	13.17	12.97
5179	548	Pb		Bullet	Ball	13.35	13.10
5170	548	Pb		Bullet	Ball	13.37	13.44
5359	548	Pb		Bullet	Ball	26.65	17.29
5261	549	Pb		Bullet	Ball	6.00	10.00
5254	549	Pb		Bullet	Ball	6.00	10.50
4304	549	Pb		Bullet	Ball	6.78	10.55
5274	549	Pb	Fe	Bullet	Ball	21.00	18.00
5258	549	Pb		Bullet	Ball	30.00	19.00
2418	550	Pb		Bullet	Ball	18.30	15.44
7457	553	Pb		Bullet	Ball	38.20	19.30
2423	554	Pb		Bullet	Ball	17.38	15.36
2980	557	Pb		Bullet	Ball	13.16	14.00
2984	569	Pb		Bullet	Ball	7.71	11.35
2987	569	Pb		Bullet	Ball	16.77	14.58
2972	579	Pb		Bullet	Ball	6.82	10.46
7357	721	Pb		Bullet	Ball	0.00	12.00
7310	721	Pb		Bullet	Ball	33.00	18.00

Find No.	Field No.	Main Material	Sub Material	Main Type	Sub Type	Weight grams	Size mm
7582	729	Pb		Bullet	Ball	0.00	15.00
2989	846	Pb		Bullet	Ball	10.69	12.49
5971	852	Pb		Bullet	Ball	12.28	13.25
5974	852	Pb		Bullet	Ball	41.05	19.89
7440	858	Pb		Bullet	Ball	0.00	13.00
7329	881	Pb		Bullet	Ball	27.00	17.00
7397	882	Pb		Bullet	Ball base of casting	0.00	13.00
7401	886	Pb		Bullet	Ball base of casting	0.00	13.00
6057	887	Pb		Bullet	Ball	10.13	12.68
6177	1028	Pb		Bullet	Ball, impacted	10.00	13.50
6775	1087	Pb		Bullet	Ball, impacted	15.00	14.00
6857	1092	Pb		Bullet	Ball, impacted	10.00	12.00
6214	1105	Pb		Bullet	Ball	25.00	17.00
6215	1105	Pb		Bullet	Ball	25.00	17.00
6321	1108	Pb		Bullet	Ball	20.00	15.50
6439	1110	Pb		Bullet	Ball	25.00	16.00
6498	1117	Pb		Bullet	Ball	5.00	10.00
6504	1117	Pb		Bullet	Ball	5.00	10.00
6506	1117	Pb		Bullet	Ball	10.00	11.00
6472	1118	Pb		Bullet	Ball	10.00	12.00

I am not suggesting that all of these lead spheres are from medieval handgunnes, but more analysis is definitely required. For example, can an 'average number of lead spheres per hectare' from areas that are confirmed 'non medieval battle areas' be compared to the number within the battle area? This then may suggest how many of the spheres might be from medieval handgunnes.

A list of 21 lead spheres recorded in the researched areas thought to be either in the battle site or campsites that are potentially from small wheeled guns (i.e. 20–38mm diameter)

Find No.	Field No.	Main Material	Sub Material	Main Type	Sub Type	Weight grams	Size mm
4737	206	Pb		Shot	Roundshot	159.00	30.00
7211	206	Pb		Shot	Roundshot	151.60	30.00
7243	206	Pb		Shot	Roundshot	161.00	30.50
1424	329	Pb		Bullet	Ball	25.03	20.34
4738	397	Pb		Shot	Roundshot	260.00	35.00
7252	398	Pb		Shot	Roundshot	67.90	22.50
4736	398	Pb		Shot	Roundshot	70.00	23.00
4786	399	Pb		Shot	Roundshot	52.00	21.00
5513	540	Pb		Shot	Roundshot	254.00	35.00
5297	542	Pb		Shot	Roundshot	53.00	20.00
5589	546	Pb	Flint	Shot	Roundshot	249.00	38.00
5613	547	Pb		Shot	Roundshot	251.00	35.00
5428	547	Pb	Flint	Shot	Roundshot	250.00	37.00
5619	547	Pb	Flint shards	Shot	Roundshot	247.00	37.00
5427	547	Pb		Shot	Roundshot	306.00	38.00
5250	548	Pb		Shot	Roundshot	125.00	28.00
5321	548	Pb		Shot	Roundshot	254.00	35.00
5386	548	Pb		Shot	Roundshot	295.00	37.00
5390	548	Pb	Flint	Shot	Roundshot	254.00	38.00
5995	550	Pb	Stone Pebble	Shot	Roundshot	297.00	37.00
5560	556	Pb	Fe	Shot	Roundshot	244.00	36.00

A list of 26 lead spheres recorded in the researched areas thought to be either in the battle site or campsites that are cannon shot (i.e. 38mm to larger diameter).

Find No.	Field No.	Main Material	Sub Material	Main Type	Sub Type	Weight grams	Size mm
7221	206	Pb		Shot	Roundshot	400.70	42.00
7213	206	Pb		Shot	Roundshot	415.20	43.00
7210	206	Pb	Flint shards	Shot	Roundshot	795.00	58.00
5729	387	Pb alloy	Fe	Shot	Roundshot	468.00	43.00

Find No.	Field No.	Main Material	Sub Material	Main Type	Sub Type	Weight grams	Size mm
4648	387	Pb		Shot	Roundshot	911.00	53.00
7231	387	Pb	Stone pebble	Shot	Roundshot	3,577.00	97.00
4733	398	Pb	Fe	Shot	Roundshot	452.00	47.00
4735	398	Pb	Flint shards	Shot	Roundshot	793.00	57.00
4734	398	Pb	Fe and flint shards	Shot	Roundshot	906.00	60.00
4889	542	Pb		Shot	Roundshot	405.00	42.00
5303	542	Pb		Shot	Roundshot	486.00	44.00
4886	542	Pb	Fe	Shot	Roundshot	656.00	50.00
5305	542	Pb	Flint chunks	Shot	Roundshot	760.00	56.00
5443	545	Pb		Shot	Roundshot	925.00	59.50
5589	546	Pb	Flint	Shot	Roundshot	249.00	38.00
5678	546	Pb		Shot	Roundshot	415.00	44.00
5427	547	Pb		Shot	Roundshot	306.00	38.00
5484	547	Pb	Flint pebble	Shot	Roundshot	674.00	57.00
5390	548	Pb	Flint	Shot	Roundshot	254.00	38.00
5385	548	Pb		Shot	Roundshot	262.00	39.00
5365	548	Pb	Stone	Shot	Roundshot	3,214.00	97.00
5992	550	Pb		Shot	Roundshot	1,127.00	65.00
5685	702	Pb	Stone pebble	Shot	Roundshot	1,066.00	63.00
7282	721	Pb		Shot	Roundshot	411.00	40.00
5718	854	Pb alloy	Fe	Shot	Roundshot	567.00	50.00
7087	1563	Pb		Shot	Roundshot	370.00	40.00

There is a total of 43 shot which can only be from medieval guns. The first roundshot found in the survey was found in Field 206. This had been found (by luck) on a 10m-grid system. Having found it, the field was re-walked twice, within months, at the now standard spacing of 2.5m. No extra balls were found. However, some seven years later, in 2016, the field was surveyed for a fourth time and amazingly a further five roundshot were found, including a 97mm diameter ball.

Why did we not find these five in any of the previous surveys? One can only assume, since it was the same team each time, we simply did not put a detector head over the balls!

However, can one assume, therefore, that for every one ball found in the original survey of 2008–10, a further five (at least) could still be in the fields? If so, we could be looking at a minimum of another 175 balls of 20mm or larger waiting to be found, giving us a total of a minimum of 218 balls!

If this extrapolation was found to be true, then I think we would really be able to start to see scatter patterns in specific sizes of balls and potentially even in make-up of the balls. Those patterns in turn might then begin to put us in a better position to work out where the guns themselves would have been. Therefore, an obvious part of the research project should be to redetect the core area on the assumption that there will be at least *some more* roundshot. A somewhat more difficult question to answer concerns the size of lead spheres and the date that they were fired.

Bibliography and Sources

Introduction
Foss, Peter, *The Field of Redemore, The Battle of Bosworth, 1485*, Kairos Press, 1998

Chapter *1*
Austin, John, *Merevale and Atherstone 1485: Recent Bosworth Discoveries*, Friends of Atherstone Heritage, 2004

Chapter 2
Crowland Chronicle
Historic England, *The Augustinian Priory of Ranton*, 1998
Jones, Michael, *Bosworth 1485: Psychology of a Battle*, John Murray, 2014
Vergil, Polydore, *Historia Anglia*, 1505
Williams, Danny, *The Battle of Bosworth*, Leicestershire Museums, Arts & Records Service, 1996

Chapter 3
The British Museum, Portable Antiquities Scheme database
Hampton, W.E., 'Opposition to Henry Tudor after Bosworth', an article first published in *The Ricardian*, December 1976 and re-published in James Petre (ed.), *Richard III: Crown & People*, Sutton Publishing, 1985
Ingram, Mike, *Bosworth 1485*, The History Press, 2012
Skidmore, Chris, *Bosworth – the Birth of the Tudors*, Orion, 2014

Chapter 4
Alchin, Linda, 'Life in a Medieval Village', 2016
Curia Regis Rolls, 1194–1272
Ekwall, Eilert, *The Concise Oxford Dictionary of English Place Names*, Oxford University Press, 1960
Holinshed's *Chronicles of England*, 1577

Chapter 5
Johnstone, John (ed.), *Memoirs of Dr Samuel Parr*, Forgotten Books, 2012
Jones, Michael, *Bosworth 1485: Psychology of a Battle*, John Murray, 2014

Chapter 6
Crowland Chonicle
Ingram, Mike, *Richard III and the Battle of Bosworth*, Helion and Company, 2019
Vergil, Polydore, *Urbinatis Anglicæ Historiæ Libri Vigintiseptem*, 1555

Chapter 7

Curry, Anne and Glenn Foard, 'Where are the Dead of Medieval Battles? A Preliminary Survey', *Journal of Conflict Archaeolgy*, Vol. 11, 2016, Issue 2–3

Ingram, Mike, *Richard III and the Battle of Bosworth*, Helion and Company, 2019

Masters, Peter, *Geophysical Survey at Bosworth Battlefield, Shenton, Leicestershire*, Cranfield Forensic Institute Report No. 018, July 2008

St Clare Byrne, Muriel (ed.), *The Lisle Letters: An Abridgement*, University of Chicago Press, 1981

Unknown, 'Song of Lady Bessy'

Chapter 8

'The Ballad of Bosworth Field'

Crowland Chronicle

Parliamentary Record, 1485, AUTHOR: King and council. TEXT: 'Rotuli Parliamentarium', ed. J. Strachey, 6 vols (London, 1767–83), VI, p. 176 (English, spelling modernised)

Shakespeare, William, *The Tragedy of King Richard III*

'Vatican Regesta', *Calendar of Papal Registers 685, 1484–1487, Calendar of Papal Registers Relating to Great Britain and Ireland, Volume 14: 1484–1492* (1960), pp. 14–30

Chapter 10

Appleby, Dr Jo, 'Perimortem trauma in King Richard III: a skeletal analysis', *The Lancet*, Vol. 385, Issue 9964, January 2015

Molinet, Jean, *Chronicles*; Molinet lived 1435–1507 and the *Chronicles* cover the period 1474–1504 but was not published until 1828 after being edited by J.A. Buchon

Chapter 12

Shakespeare, William, *The Tragedy of King Richard III*

Chapter 14

'The gauge of firearms', wikipedia.org

Ross, David, 'The Battle of Barnet', https://www.britainexpress.com/History/battles/barnet.htm

Chapter 15

Ingram, Mike, *Richard III and the Battle of Bosworth*, Helion and Company, 2019

Index

Page numbers in bold refer to images